casual cooking

One pot stop

casual cooking

One pot
stop

LOVE FOOD™

This edition published by Parragon Books Ltd in 2014
LOVE FOOD is an imprint of Parragon Books Ltd

Parragon Books Ltd
Chartist House
15–17 Trim Street
Bath BA1 1HA, UK
www.parragon.com/lovefood

ISBN 978-1-4723-8488-1

Printed in China

Cover photography by Charlie Richards
Designed by Beth Kalynka
Nutritional analysis by Judith Wills

Notes for the Reader
This book uses both metric and imperial measurements. Follow the same units of
measurement throughout; do not mix metric and imperial. All spoon measurements are
level: teaspoons are assumed to be 5 ml, and tablespoons are assumed to be 15 ml. Unless
otherwise stated, milk is assumed to be full fat, eggs and individual vegetables are medium,
and pepper is freshly ground black pepper. Unless otherwise stated, all root vegetables should
be peeled prior to using.

Garnishes, decorations and serving suggestions are all optional and not necessarily included
in the recipe ingredients or method. Any optional ingredients and seasoning to taste are not
included in the nutritional analysis. The times given are an approximate guide only. Preparation
times differ according to the techniques used by different people and the cooking times may
also vary from those given. Optional ingredients, variations or serving suggestions have not
been included in the time calculations. Nutritional values are per serving (Serves...) or
per item (Makes...).

contents

chicken feed

Always ensure poultry is thoroughly cooked and tender before serving. Poultry should be piping hot and the juices should run clear with no trace of pinkness when a skewer or the tip of a sharp knife is inserted into the thickest part of the meat.

a batch made in heaven

Cook recipes in bulk and freeze to create a fabulous supply of home-cooked meals that simply need defrosting and heating to enjoy. The perfect solution for when time is tight — or cooking just isn't on your agenda!

a poultry excuse

chicken soup with leeks & rice	8
chicken wings	10
turkey steaks with a chilli-maple glaze	12
chicken with jerusalem artichokes	14
turkey with a cranberry glaze	16
chicken & cashew nuts	18
turkey meatballs with a spicy-honey glaze	20
chicken with creamed shallots	22
coq au vin	24
POTS OF CHOICE	26
moroccan-style turkey	28
chicken stew	30
chicken jalfrezi	32
duck stew with pancetta & olives	34
mustard-crusted turkey breast	36
boned & stuffed roast duck	38
chicken braised with baby vegetables	40
roast chicken	42

chicken soup with leeks & rice

prep: 15-20 mins, plus cooling
cook: 35-40 mins

2 tbsp olive oil

3 leeks, chopped

6 skinless, boneless chicken thighs, diced

55 g/2 oz long-grain rice

1.3 litres/2¼ pints vegetable stock

dash of Worcestershire sauce

6 fresh chives, snipped

6 thin bacon rashers

2 tbsp chopped fresh parsley

salt and pepper

top tip

If you're short of time, use left-over cooked and shredded chicken and shop-bought cooked crispy bacon.

1. Heat the oil in a saucepan. Add the leeks and cook over a low heat, stirring occasionally, for 5 minutes, until softened. Add the chicken, increase the heat to medium and cook, stirring frequently, for 2 minutes. Add the rice and cook, stirring constantly, for a further 2 minutes.

2. Pour in the stock, add the Worcestershire sauce and chives and bring to the boil. Reduce the heat, cover and simmer for 20–25 minutes. Check the chicken is tender and cooked through. Meanwhile, preheat the grill.

3. Grill the bacon for 2–4 minutes on each side, until crisp. Remove and leave to cool, then crumble.

4. Season the soup with salt and pepper to taste and stir in the parsley. Ladle into serving bowls, sprinkle with the crumbled bacon and serve immediately.

serves 6

cals: 288   fat: 14.1g   sat fat: 4.2g   fibre: 1.1g   carbs: 15.3g   sugar: 2.4g   salt: 4.2g   protein: 26g

chicken wings

prep: 25 mins
cook: 40-60 mins

2 tbsp plain flour

¼ tsp hot paprika

24 chicken wings, trimmed

2 tbsp olive oil, plus extra if needed

4 spicy Italian sausages,
  cut into 4-cm/1½-inch pieces

1 onion, thinly sliced

2 red peppers, deseeded and sliced

4 pickled cherry peppers, sliced

4 garlic cloves, sliced

125 ml/4 fl oz chicken stock

125 ml/4 fl oz dry white wine

2 tbsp lemon juice

pinch of dried chilli flakes (optional)

salt and pepper

4 tbsp chopped fresh flat-leaf parsley,
  to garnish

1. Mix together the flour and paprika in a wide dish. Season the chicken wings with salt and pepper, then dredge them in the flour mixture, shaking off the excess.

2. Heat the oil in a large, deep frying pan over a medium–high heat. Add as many chicken wings as will fit in the pan in a single layer, and fry for 3–5 minutes, until golden brown on both sides. Remove from the pan and set aside. Add extra oil to the pan, if needed, and repeat until all the wings are fried.

3. Pour off all but 1 tablespoon of the oil. Add the sausages to the pan and fry for 3–5 minutes, until brown all over. Remove from the pan and set aside.

4. Pour off all but 1 tablespoon of the oil from the pan. Add the onion and red peppers and stir for 3–5 minutes, until soft. Add the cherry peppers and garlic and stir for a further 2 minutes, until the garlic is soft.

5. Return the chicken and sausages to the pan. Stir in the stock, wine, lemon juice and chilli flakes, (if using), and season with salt and pepper. Bring to the boil, cover the pan, reduce the heat to low and simmer for 15–20 minutes, until the wings are cooked through and the juices run clear when you cut into one.

6. Using a slotted spoon, transfer the wings, sausages, red peppers and cherry peppers to warmed plates. Bring the liquid in the pan to the boil, then spoon over the meat. Garnish with parsley and serve immediately.

serves 4

cals: 940   fat: 65.2g   sat fat: 18.7g   fibre: 2.5g   carbs: 17.4g   sugar: 4.8g   salt: 2.7g   protein: 62g

turkey steaks with a chilli-maple glaze

prep: 20 mins
cook: 12-15 mins

4 turkey breast steaks, about
   125 g/4½ oz each

2 tbsp olive oil

1 garlic clove, crushed

4 tbsp maple syrup

2 tbsp tomato purée

2 tbsp Worcestershire sauce

3 tbsp lime juice

1½ tsp hot chilli sauce

salt and pepper

mashed potato, to serve (optional)

2 tbsp chopped fresh flat-leaf parsley,
   to garnish

top tip

If you don't have a rolling pin, flatten each steak with the bottom of a heavy saucepan, taking care to ensure the breasts are an even thickness all over.

1. Place the turkey breasts between two pieces of clingfilm and beat with a rolling pin until very thin. Season to taste with salt and pepper.

2. Heat the oil in a large frying pan, add the turkey and fry over a fairly high heat, turning once, for 3–4 minutes until golden brown.

3. Mix together the garlic, maple syrup, tomato purée, Worcestershire sauce, lime juice and chilli sauce, then spoon over the turkey.

4. Turn the turkey in the glaze to coat, then reduce the heat to low, cover the pan and cook very gently for 8–10 minutes until the turkey is tender and thoroughly cooked.

5. Adjust the seasoning to taste, sprinkle with parsley and serve immediately with mashed potato, if liked.

cals: 301   fat: 7.9g   sat fat: 1g   fibre: 0.6g   carbs: 18.5g   sugar: 14.8g   salt: 2g   protein: 37.7g

chicken with jerusalem artichokes

25 g/1 oz butter

1 onion, finely chopped

200 g/7 oz Jerusalem artichokes, sliced

200 ml/7 fl oz water

100 ml/3½ fl oz white wine

2 fresh tarragon sprigs or ½ tsp dried tarragon

2 skinless, boneless chicken breasts, about 115 g/4 oz each

1 tsp Dijon mustard

3 tbsp crème fraîche

salt and pepper

chopped fresh tarragon, to garnish (optional)

cooked rice, to serve (optional)

1. Melt the butter in a large frying pan over a medium heat, add the onion and cook for 4–5 minutes, or until soft. Add the artichokes, water, wine and tarragon.

2. Bring to the boil, then reduce the heat and simmer, covered, for 5 minutes, or until the artichokes are just tender.

3. Cut each chicken breast into 4 pieces and add to the pan. Season with salt and pepper and continue to cook, stirring, for 10 minutes, or until the chicken is cooked through and shows no traces of pink.

4. Remove the tarragon sprigs and stir in the mustard and crème fraîche. Increase the heat and leave the sauce to bubble and thicken. Divide between two warmed plates and garnish with chopped tarragon, if using. Serve immediately with cooked rice, if liked.

cals: 443   fat: 21.4g   sat fat: 12.5g   fibre: 3.2g   carbs: 26.9g   sugar: 13.9g   salt: 2.1g   protein: 28.1g

turkey with a cranberry glaze

prep: 15 mins
cook: 10-12 mins

450 g/1 lb skinless, boneless
   turkey breast
2 tbsp sunflower oil
15 g/½ oz stem ginger, in syrup
50 g/1¾ oz fresh or frozen cranberries
100 g/3½ oz canned chestnuts
4 tbsp cranberry sauce
3 tbsp light soy sauce
salt and pepper

1. Using a sharp knife, thinly slice the turkey breast.

2. Heat the oil in a large preheated wok or frying pan. Add the turkey and stir-fry for 5 minutes, or until cooked through. Drain the syrup from the stem ginger. Using a sharp knife, finely chop the ginger and add to the wok along with the cranberries. Stir-fry for 2–3 minutes, or until the cranberries are soft.

3. Add the chestnuts, cranberry sauce and soy sauce, season to taste with salt and pepper and leave to bubble for 2–3 minutes.

4. Transfer to warmed serving dishes and serve immediately.

variation

Chicken is the obvious substitute for turkey, if preferred. Any cut of the meat can be used, not just the breast meat

cals: 293   fat: 14.4g   sat fat: 1g   fibre: 1.9g   carbs: 19.2g   sugar: 10.5g   salt: 2.6g   protein: 29.6g

chicken & cashew nuts

prep: 15-20 mins, plus soaking and marinating
cook: 12-15 mins

450 g/1 lb chicken breast meat

3 dried Chinese mushrooms, soaked in warm water for 20 minutes

2 tbsp vegetable oil or groundnut oil

4 slices fresh ginger

1 tsp finely chopped garlic

1 red pepper, deseeded and cut into 2.5-cm/1-inch squares

1 tbsp light soy sauce

85 g/3 oz cashew nuts, toasted

marinade

2 tbsp light soy sauce

1 tsp Chinese rice wine

pinch of sugar

1. Cut the chicken into cubes and put in a dish. Combine the marinade ingredients and pour over the chicken. Leave to marinate for at least 20 minutes.

2. Squeeze any excess water from the mushrooms and finely slice, discarding any tough stems. Reserve the soaking water.

3. Heat a wok over a high heat, then add 1 tablespoon of oil. Add the ginger and stir-fry until fragrant. Stir in the chicken and cook for 2 minutes, until it turns golden brown. Before the chicken is cooked through, remove and set aside.

4. Wipe out the wok with kitchen paper. Heat the wok over a high heat and add the remaining oil. Add the garlic and cook, stirring, for 1 minute. Add the mushrooms and red pepper and stir-fry for a further 2 minutes. Add about 2 tablespoons of the mushroom soaking water and cook for about 2 minutes, or until the water has evaporated.

5. Return the chicken to the wok, add the soy sauce and the cashew nuts and stir-fry for 2 minutes. Cut into the middle of the chicken to check there are no remaining traces of pink. Serve immediately.

serves 4

cals: 334   fat: 19.1g   sat fat: 3g   fibre: 1.7g   carbs: 11.1g   sugar: 2.6g   salt: 2g   protein: 30g

turkey meatballs with a spicy-honey glaze

prep: 20-25 mins
cook: 20 mins

olive oil, for greasing and brushing

675 g/1 lb 8 oz fresh turkey mince

½ yellow onion, finely diced

25 g/1 oz fresh breadcrumbs

3 garlic cloves, finely chopped

2 tsp dried oregano

¾ tsp salt

¾ tsp pepper

roasted vegetables and freshly cooked rice, to serve (optional)

glaze

4 tbsp clear honey

2 tbsp tomato ketchup

1 tbsp cider vinegar

¼–½ tsp ground chipotle chilli

3. Meanwhile, prepare the glaze. Put the honey, ketchup, vinegar and chilli into a bowl and stir to combine.

4. Remove the meatballs from the oven and increase the oven temperature to 230°C/450°F/Gas Mark 8.

1. Preheat the oven to 190°C/375°F/Gas Mark 5 and brush a large baking dish with oil.

2. In a large bowl, combine the mince, onion, breadcrumbs, garlic, oregano, salt and pepper and mix well to combine. Form the mixture into 4-cm/1½-inch balls and place them in the prepared dish. Brush the tops and sides of the meatballs with olive oil. Bake in the preheated oven for about 15 minutes.

5. Pour off as much liquid as you can from the baking dish. Spoon the glaze over the meatballs, making sure they all get some sauce. Return to the oven and bake for a further 5 minutes, or until the glaze is reduced.

6. Serve immediately with roasted vegetables and freshly cooked rice, if liked.

serves 4

cals: 415   fat: 21.1g   sat fat: 4.6g   fibre: 0.7g   carbs: 25g   sugar: 20.5g   salt: 1.5g   protein: 32.9g

chicken with creamed shallots

prep: 20 mins
cook: 1 hour 5 mins

1 whole chicken, cut into quarters

1 tbsp unsalted butter

1 tbsp olive oil

225 g/8 oz shallots, peeled and cut in thick 1-cm/½-inch slices

2 tbsp plain flour

50 ml/2 fl oz white wine

225 ml/8 fl oz chicken stock

50 ml/2 fl oz double cream

1 tbsp snipped fresh chives

salt and pepper

top tip

You can either serve this beautifully indulgent dish with mashed potatoes and greens – or simply fresh crusty bread for soaking up the creamy sauce.

1. Generously season the chicken with salt and pepper on both sides. Heat the butter and oil in a casserole over a medium–high heat. Add the chicken and sear for about 4 minutes on each side. Transfer to a plate and add the shallots to the casserole. Reduce the heat and cook for 5 minutes, or until golden. Add the flour and stir in. Cook for 2 minutes.

2. Add the wine and stock and bring to the boil, scraping any sediment from the base of the casserole. Return the chicken to the casserole. Cover tightly, and simmer over a low heat for about 40 minutes, until the chicken is cooked through.

3. Transfer the chicken to a serving platter and loosely cover with foil. Increase the heat to high, add the cream, bring to the boil and cook for 5 minutes, or until reduced and slightly thickened. Add the chives, and salt and pepper to taste. Pour the sauce over the chicken, and serve immediately.

cals: 534   fat: 38.6g   sat fat: 13.6g   fibre: 1.1g   carbs: 8.6g   sugar: 2.3g   salt: 2.3g   protein: 34.1g

coq au vin

prep: 20 mins
cook: 30 mins

30 g/1 oz plain flour

4 skinned chicken leg quarters
(drumstick and thigh)

2 tbsp olive oil

2 bacon rashers, diced

1 shallot, diced

2 carrots, diced

225 g/8 oz button mushrooms, diced

300 ml/10 fl oz chicken stock

175 ml/6 fl oz red wine

1 tbsp tomato purée

3–4 fresh thyme sprigs

salt and pepper

fresh crusty bread, to serve (optional)

top tip

Use a full-bodied red wine, such as Burgundy, for this delicious take on the French classic.

1. Put the flour into a wide bowl. Season the chicken all over with salt and pepper, then dip it in the flour. Reserve the remaining flour.

2. Heat the oil in a large, heavy-based frying pan over a medium–high heat. Add the chicken and cook for 3 minutes until the underside is well browned. Turn and add the bacon, shallot, carrots and mushrooms to the pan with ½ teaspoon of salt. Cook for 2–3 minutes, stirring occasionally, until the vegetables begin to soften.

3. Add the stock, wine, tomato purée and thyme to the pan and bring to the boil. Reduce the heat to low, cover the pan and cook for about 15 minutes until the chicken is cooked through. Remove the chicken from the pan and place it on a serving platter.

4. Bring the sauce to the boil, then stir 1–2 tablespoons into the reserved flour to make a paste. Transfer the paste to the sauce and cook over a medium heat, stirring, for about 2 minutes until the sauce thickens. Spoon the sauce over the chicken and serve immediately with fresh crusty bread, if liked.

serves 4

cals: 382   fat: 14.6g   sat fat: 3.2g   fibre: 2.3g   carbs: 16.2g   sugar: 5.8g   salt: 2.2g   protein: 40g

pots of choice

There are numerous vessels that are used in one-pot cooking – including woks, tagines and frying pans, as well as the commonly associated casserole. See below for a list of the most popular items and familiarize yourself with their individual uses.

Casserole

A casserole is ideal for leisurely stews and braises cooked either on the hob or in the oven, and for pot-roasting boned and rolled joints of meat. Poultry thighs and drumsticks and dense-fleshed root vegetables are good too. The moist heat encourages an exchange of flavours between meat, vegetables and seasonings, resulting in truly succulent dishes. After an hour or two with the lid on,

test by prodding with a skewer. Meat should feel meltingly tender and root vegetables should be soft but not disintegrating.

High-sided frying pan

With a tight-fitting lid and heavy ground base, a high-sided pan is perfect for slow-cooked rice dishes such as paella or risotto, and for braising larger items like chicken quarters or a joint of beef. The generous surface area provides maximum contact with heat, allowing meat to brown quickly before adding other ingredients. The contents can then be covered and left to cook at a leisurely pace.

Wok

Because of the wok's conical shape and continuous stirring, the food continually falls back to the centre where the heat is at its most intense. Since the ingredients are constantly on the move, much less fat is needed, making this a healthy way of cooking. It is very important to preheat the wok. You should be able to feel the heat radiating from it when you hold your hand flat above the base of the interior. Add the oil only when the wok is really hot. It is essential to have all the ingredients prepared, ready to add to the wok the minute the oil is at the right heat. It should be almost, but not quite, smoking.

Roasting tin

A good solid roasting tin is ideal for a joint of meat or poultry cooked alongside vegetables such as onions, potatoes, and parsnips. Orange-fleshed vegetables are particularly delicious - try carrots, pumpkin and sweet potato. Make sure the vegetables are cut into similar-sized pieces so that they cook evenly. Tuck some under the meat for extra flavour. A little stock, wine or water is all that's needed to keep everything moist. Some roasting tins are self-basting. They have dimpled lids that encourage moisture to gather and drip evenly over the contents below, resulting in a particularly succulent dish. A tin that is sturdy enough to use on the hob means you can

speed up the cooking by giving the meat a quick sizzle before it goes into the oven. The caramelized sediment will dissolve and flavour the other ingredients once they give up their liquid.

Baking and gratin dishes

These dishes are for food that is baked in the oven with a browned topping of potato, bubbling cheese, or crunchy breadcrumbs – or all three. Baking dishes are particularly suitable for one pot meals as they can be brought straight from oven to table, saving on the washing up. They are usually made in attractive shapes and colours.

moroccan-style turkey

prep: 20 mins
cook: 45-50 mins

400 g/14 oz skinless, boneless turkey breasts, diced

1 onion, sliced

1 tsp ground cumin

½ tsp ground cinnamon

1 tsp hot chilli sauce

240 g/8½ oz canned chickpeas, drained and rinsed

600 ml/1 pint chicken stock

12 dried apricots

40 g/1½ oz cornflour

75 ml/2½ fl oz cold water

2 tbsp chopped fresh coriander

cooked couscous, to serve (optional)

1. Put the turkey, onion, cumin, cinnamon, chilli sauce, chickpeas and stock into a large saucepan. Bring to the boil, reduce the heat, cover and simmer for 15 minutes.

2. Stir in the apricots and return to the boil. Reduce the heat, cover and simmer for a further 15 minutes, or until the turkey is cooked through.

3. Blend the cornflour with the water in a small bowl and stir into the casserole. Return to the boil, stirring constantly, and cook until the casserole thickens. Reduce the heat, cover and simmer for a further 5 minutes.

4. Stir half of the coriander into the casserole. Transfer to a warmed serving dish and sprinkle over the remaining coriander. Serve immediately with couscous, if liked.

1

variation

Try serving baked sweet potatoes with this casserole instead of the couscous. Their flavour will complement the spicy sweetness of the dish.

cals: 251   fat: 2.1g   sat fat: 0.7g   fibre: 3.7g   carbs: 30.4g   sugar: 7.4g   salt: 1.5g   protein: 27.9g

chicken stew

prep: 20-25 mins
cook: 35-40 mins

1 tbsp plain flour

4 skinless, boneless chicken breasts, about 140 g/5 oz each, trimmed of all visible fat and cut into 2-cm/¾-inch cubes

1 tbsp sunflower or corn oil

8 baby onions

2 garlic cloves, crushed

225 ml/8 fl oz chicken stock

2 carrots, diced

2 celery sticks, diced

225 g/8 oz frozen peas

1 yellow pepper, deseeded and diced

115 g/4 oz button mushrooms, sliced

125 ml/4 fl oz low-fat natural yogurt

3 tbsp chopped fresh flat-leaf parsley

salt and white pepper

1. Spread out the flour on a dish and season with salt and pepper. Add the chicken and, using your hands, coat in the flour.

2. Heat the oil in a large casserole. Add the onions and garlic and cook over a low heat, stirring occasionally, for 5 minutes. Add the chicken and cook, stirring, for 10 minutes, or until just beginning to colour.

3. Gradually stir in the stock, then add the carrots, celery and peas. Bring to the boil, then reduce the heat, cover and simmer for 5 minutes. Add the yellow pepper and the mushrooms, cover and simmer for a further 10 minutes until the chicken is cooked through and no traces of pink remain.

4. Stir in the yogurt and chopped parsley and season to taste with salt and pepper. Cook for 1–2 minutes, or until heated through, then serve immediately.

cals: 329   fat: 8.5g   sat fat: 1.7g   fibre: 6.2g   carbs: 26g   sugar: 11.4g   salt: 2g   protein: 37.2g

chicken jalfrezi

prep: 20 mins
cook: 30-35 mins

55 g/2 oz ghee or 4 tbsp vegetable oil
or groundnut oil

8 skinless, boneless chicken
thighs, sliced

1 large onion, chopped

2 tbsp garlic paste

2 tbsp ginger paste

2 green peppers, deseeded and chopped

1 large fresh green chilli,
deseeded and finely chopped

1 tsp ground cumin

1 tsp ground coriander

¼–½ tsp chilli powder

½ tsp ground turmeric

¼ tsp salt

400 g/14 oz canned chopped tomatoes

125 ml/4 fl oz water

2 tbsp chopped fresh coriander, to
garnish

1. Melt half the ghee in a wok or large frying pan over a medium-high heat. Add the chicken pieces and stir for around 5 minutes until browned, but not necessarily cooked through, then remove from the pan with a slotted spoon and set aside.

2. Melt the remaining ghee in the pan. Add the onion and fry, stirring frequently, for 5–8 minutes until golden brown. Stir in the garlic and ginger paste and continue frying for 2 minutes, stirring frequently.

3. Add the peppers to the pan and stir for around 2 minutes.

4. Stir in the chilli, cumin, coriander, chilli powder, turmeric and salt. Add the tomatoes with their juices and the water and bring to the boil.

5. Reduce the heat to low, add the chicken and leave to simmer, uncovered, for 10 minutes, stirring frequently, until the peppers are tender and the chicken is cooked through. Garnish with the coriander and serve immediately.

cals: 387   fat: 20.7g   sat fat: 3.5g   fibre: 2.3g   carbs: 13g   sugar: 6.6g   salt: 0.8g   protein: 34g

duck stew with pancetta & olives

prep: 20 mins
cook: 1¼ hours–1 hour 20 mins

2 tbsp olive oil

1.8 kg/4 lb oven-ready duck, cut into 8 pieces

150 g/5½ oz pancetta, diced

1 large onion, diced

1 celery stick, diced

1 carrot, diced

1 garlic clove, crushed

175 ml/6 fl oz red wine

400 ml/14 fl oz passata

1 fresh red chilli, finely chopped

3 fresh rosemary sprigs

12 black olives

salt and pepper

2 tbsp chopped fresh flat-leaf parsley, to garnish

1. Heat the oil in a large saucepan and fry the duck pieces, in batches, until golden brown. Remove and set aside.

2. Tip out all but 1 tablespoon of the oil and fry the pancetta, stirring, until golden. Add the onion, celery, carrot and garlic and fry gently, stirring, for 3–4 minutes.

3. Stir in the wine and boil for 1 minute, then add the passata, chilli, rosemary and olives and season to taste with salt and pepper.

4. Return the duck pieces to the pan, spooning over the sauce to cover. Cover and simmer gently for about 1 hour, or until the duck is tender. Sprinkle with the chopped parsley and serve immediately.

top tip

Simply omit the red chilli if you don't like a spicy kick to your food. If you are unsure, add chilli flakes, a little at a time, until you reach the desired heat level.

cals: 894   fat: 69g   sat fat: 22.1g   fibre: 3.1g   carbs: 16.7g   sugar: 10.2g   salt: 3g   protein: 42g

mustard-crusted turkey breast

prep: 20 mins
cook: 40 mins, plus resting

1 x 650 g/1 lb 7 oz turkey breast joint,
   skin removed

25 g/1 oz fresh white breadcrumbs
   (preferably ciabatta)

40 g/1½ oz butter, softened

2 tbsp wholegrain mustard

1 tbsp finely chopped fresh rosemary

1 garlic clove, crushed

1 tbsp fresh lemon juice

salt and pepper

fresh rosemary sprigs, to garnish

1. Preheat the oven to 190°C/375°F/
Gas Mark 5. Place the turkey in a small
roasting tin and season with salt and pepper.

2. Mix the breadcrumbs, butter, mustard,
rosemary, garlic and lemon juice together
to make a thick paste. Season with salt
and pepper.

3. Spread the mustard mixture over the
surface of the turkey, pressing out with your
fingers to make an even crust.

4. Cook the turkey in the preheated oven for
about 40 minutes, until golden brown and
thoroughly cooked – the juices should run
clear when the thickest part of the meat is
pierced with a sharp knife.

5. Remove from the oven, loosely cover with
foil and leave to stand for about 10 minutes.
Serve sliced, with the pan juices spooned over.
Garnish with fresh rosemary sprigs.

top tip

If the joint is rolled and tied,
it's best to untie before coating
with the mustard crust.

cals: 289   fat: 10.3g   sat fat: 5.6g   fibre: 0.9g   carbs: 4.8g   sugar: 1g   salt: 2.2g   protein: 41.6g

boned & stuffed roast duck

prep: 30-35 mins
cook: 1½-2 hours

1.8 kg/4 lb duck (dressed weight), ask your butcher to bone the duck and cut off the wings at the first joint

450 g/1 lb flavoured sausage meat, such as pork and apricot

1 small onion, finely chopped

1 Cox's apple, cored and finely chopped

85 g/3 oz ready-to-eat dried apricots, finely chopped

85 g/3 oz chopped walnuts

2 tbsp chopped fresh parsley

1 large or 2 smaller duck breasts, skin removed

salt and pepper

ready-made apricot sauce, to serve (optional)

top tip

As well as asking your butcher to bone and cut the meat, you can ask them to stuff it with good-quality sausage meat too, saving you valuable time in the kitchen.

1. Wipe the duck inside and out with kitchen paper. Lay it on a board, skin-side down, and season well with salt and pepper.

2. Mix the sausage meat, onion, apple, apricots, walnuts and parsley together and season well with salt and pepper. Form into a large sausage shape. Lay the duck breast on the whole duck and cover with the stuffing. Wrap the whole duck around the filling and tuck in any leg and neck flaps.

3. Preheat the oven to 190°C/375°F/Gas Mark 5. Sew the duck up the back and across both ends with fine string. Mould the duck into a good shape and place, sewn-side down, on a wire rack over a roasting tin. Roast in the preheated oven for 1½–2 hours, basting occasionally, until golden brown and crispy.

4. Carve the duck into thick slices at the table and serve immediately with apricot sauce, if using.

cals: 774   fat: 57.2g   sat fat: 17.4g   fibre: 4g   carbs: 23.3g   sugar: 13.7g   salt: 2.3g   protein: 41.9g

chicken braised with baby vegetables

prep: 15 mins
cook: 30–35 mins

4 skinless, boneless chicken breasts

15 g/½ oz butter

1 tbsp olive oil

8 shallots

275 ml/9 fl oz chicken stock

12 baby carrots

8 baby turnips

2 bay leaves

140 g/5 oz fresh or frozen peas

salt and pepper

new potatoes, to serve (optional)

top tip

Bay leaves impart a bittersweet, pungent flavour that enhances many dishes. Just remember to remove them prior to serving as they're not so pleasant to eat due to their tough nature.

1. Cut deep slashes through the chicken at intervals and sprinkle with salt and pepper.

2. Heat the butter and oil in a wide, flameproof casserole or saucepan, add the chicken breasts and shallots and fry, turning, for 3–4 minutes until golden brown.

3. Add the stock and bring to the boil, then add the carrots, turnips and bay leaves. Reduce the heat, cover and simmer gently for 20 minutes.

4. Stir in the peas and cook for a further 5 minutes. Check the chicken and vegetables are tender and the juices of the meat run clear when a skewer is inserted into the thickest part of the meat.

5. Remove and discard the bay leaves, adjust the seasoning to taste and serve immediately with new potatoes, if liked.

cals: 294   fat: 11g   sat fat: 3.5g   fibre: 4.3g   carbs: 12.6g   sugar: 6.9g   salt: 1.9g   protein: 35.3g

roast chicken

prep: 25 mins
cook: 2 hours 5 mins, plus resting

1 chicken, weighing 2.25 kg/5 lb
55 g/2 oz butter, softened
2 tbsp chopped fresh lemon thyme,
   plus extra sprigs to garnish (optional)
1 lemon, cut into quarters
125 ml/4 fl oz white wine,
   plus extra if needed
salt and pepper

1. Preheat the oven to 220°C/425°F/Gas Mark 7. Place the chicken in a roasting tin. Put the butter in a bowl, then mix in the thyme, and salt and pepper to taste and use to butter the chicken.

2. Place the lemon inside the cavity. Pour the wine over and roast in the preheated oven for 15 minutes.

3. Reduce the temperature to 190°C/375°F/Gas Mark 5 and roast, basting frequently, for a further 1¾ hours.

4. To check a whole bird is cooked through, pierce the thickest part of the leg between the drumstick and the thigh with a thin skewer. Any juices should be piping hot and clear with no traces of red or pink. To further check, gently pull the leg away from the body, the leg should 'give' and no traces of pinkness or blood should remain. Transfer to a warmed platter, cover with foil and allow to rest for 10 minutes.

5. Place the roasting tin on the hob and simmer the pan juices gently over a low heat until they have reduced and are thick and glossy. Season and reserve.

6. To carve the chicken, place on a clean chopping board. Using a carving knife and fork, cut between the wings and the side of the breast. Remove the wings and cut slices off the breast.

7. Cut the legs from the body and cut through the joint to make drumsticks and thigh portions. Serve with the pan juices, garnished with extra thyme sprigs, if liked.

top tip

Try to buy a good quality fresh chicken as opposed to a frozen bird. Frozen chickens do not retain the same flavour as fresh meat.

serves 6

cals: 441   fat: 27.7g   sat fat: 10.3g   fibre: 0.3g   carbs: 1.6g   sugar: 0.5g   salt: 1.5g   protein: 41g

making ends meat

Cooking with meat needn't be expensive. Cheaper cuts are ideal for slow cooking methods and can make rich and robust stews and casseroles with magically transformed tender, melt-in-the-mouth meats that prove hard to resist!

we'll meat again

salt pork & lentil soup

prep: 20 mins
cook: 2 hours 5 mins–2 hours 35 mins

225 g/8 oz salt pork, diced

2 tbsp olive oil

1 onion, chopped

3 garlic cloves, finely chopped

4 potatoes, diced

500 g/1 lb 2 oz red lentils

2 litres/3½ pints vegetable stock

1 bouquet garni (1 bay leaf, 1 fresh
    thyme sprig and 3 fresh parsley
    sprigs, tied together)

salt and pepper

fresh crusty bread, to serve (optional)

variation

Add 150 g/5½ oz chopped red cabbage along with the salt pork in step 3 for a different taste and texture. Ensure the cabbage is cooked to your taste before serving.

1. Put the salt pork into a large saucepan and cook over medium heat, stirring frequently, for 8–10 minutes, until it has released most of its fat and is browned all over. Remove from the pan with a slotted spoon and drain on kitchen paper. Set aside.

2. Add the oil to the pan and heat. Add the onion, garlic and potatoes and cook over a low heat, stirring occasionally, for 5 minutes, until the onion has softened. Stir in the lentils and cook, stirring constantly, for 5 minutes.

3. Pour in the stock, increase the heat to medium, add the bouquet garni and bring to the boil, stirring constantly. Reduce the heat, cover and simmer for 1½–2 hours, until the lentils are very soft. Stir in the salt pork, season to taste with salt and pepper, and cook, stirring occasionally, for a further 10 minutes, until heated through.

4. Remove the pan from the heat. Remove and discard the bouquet garni. Pour the soup into warmed bowls and serve immediately with fresh crusty bread, if liked.

cals: 678   fat: 38.6g   sat fat: 13.3g   fibre: 11g   carbs: 63.2g   sugar: 2.4g   salt: 5g   protein: 24.4g

chorizo & blue cheese omelette

prep: 15 mins, plus cooling
cook: 20 mins

1 tbsp olive oil
1 tbsp butter
200 g/7 oz chorizo, diced
1 large red onion, chopped
5 large eggs, beaten
150 g/5½ oz blue cheese, crumbled
pepper

1. Preheat the grill to high.

2. Heat the oil and butter in a large fying pan over a medium heat. Add the chorizo and red onion and fry, stirring, for 8–10 minutes, or until golden.

3. Pour in the eggs and season to taste with pepper. Using a spatula, scrape the eggs away from the edges of the pan in a circular motion until the omelette starts to set.

4. Scatter over the cheese and place under the preheated grill for 5 minutes, or until golden and bubbling.

5. Remove from the grill and leave to cool for 5 minutes before serving.

cals: 1102   fat: 87.9g   sat fat: 38.1g   fibre: 2g   carbs: 14.6g   sugar: 5.3g   salt: 6.4g   protein: 61.3g

italian sausage subs

prep: 15–20 mins
cook: 30–35 mins

2 tbsp olive oil

8 Italian sausages

1 green pepper

1 red pepper

1 orange pepper

1 onion

2 garlic cloves

½ tsp salt

½ tsp pepper

125 ml/4 fl oz red wine

425 g/15 oz canned chopped tomatoes

2 tsp dried oregano

4 submarine rolls

salad

280 g/10 oz rocket

3 tbsp red wine vinegar

½ tsp salt

¼ tsp pepper

4 tbsp olive oil

1. Heat the oil in a large frying pan over a medium–high heat. Add the sausages and cook, turning occasionally, for 6–8 minutes until brown all over. Remove from the pan and set aside. Meanwhile, deseed the green, red and orange peppers and slice them into 2.5-cm/1-inch wide strips. Halve the onion and thinly slice into half-circles. Finely chop the garlic.

2. Add the vegetables to the pan and cook, stirring frequently, for about 4 minutes until they begin to soften, then add the garlic, salt and pepper. Cook, stirring, for a further 1–2 minutes. Add the wine, tomatoes and oregano and bring to the boil. Return the sausages to the pan, cover and cook for about 15 minutes until the sausages are cooked through.

3. Meanwhile, put the rocket into a bowl. Put the vinegar, salt and pepper into a small bowl, then slowly whisk in the oil. Toss the dressing with the rocket.

4. Split the rolls and place two sausages on each. Spoon the vegetables and sauce over the top. Serve hot with the salad on the side.

makes 4

cals: 757   fat: 38g   sat fat: 8.6g   fibre: 5.8g   carbs: 60.5g   sugar: 11.7g   salt: 3.5g   protein: 39.3g

pork stir-fry with cashews & lime

prep: 20-25 mins
cook: 10 mins

variation

For those who don't like the strong taste of mint, simply replace with fresh basil leaves instead, for a milder, yet equally delicious garnish.

280 g/10 oz pork fillet

1 lime

1 tsp coriander seeds

½ tsp white peppercorns

¼ tsp salt

¼ tsp sugar

3 spring onions

1 garlic clove

2.5 cm/1-inch piece fresh ginger

1 small green pepper

2 tbsp cashew nuts

2 tbsp groundnut oil

1 tbsp chicken stock

1 tsp Thai fish sauce

2 tbsp fresh mint, to garnish

1. Slice the pork diagonally across the grain into thin bite-sized pieces. Cover in clingfilm and flatten with a mallet. Zest and juice the lime. Using a mortar and pestle, crush together the coriander seeds, peppercorns, salt, sugar and lime rind. Remove the clingfilm from the meat and press the mixture onto both sides of the pork. Separate the white and green parts of the spring onions, halve lengthways and slice into 2-cm/¾-inch pieces.

2. Thinly slice the garlic and finely chop the ginger. Deseed and thinly slice the green pepper. Roughly chop the nuts.

3. Heat a wok over a high heat, then add 1 tablespoon of the oil. Add the pork and stir-fry for 2–3 minutes until the pork is cooked through. Transfer to a plate with the juices. Wipe out the wok, reheat over a medium–high heat, add the remaining oil, the garlic and ginger and stir-fry for a few seconds. Add the white spring onion and green pepper and stir-fry for 2 minutes. Add the nuts and stir-fry for 1 minute.

4. Increase the heat to high, then return the pork and juices to the wok. Add the stock, lime juice, fish sauce and the green spring onion. Stir-fry for 30 seconds, sprinkle with mint and serve immediately.

cals: 314   fat: 14.8g   sat fat: 2.4g   fibre: 3g   carbs: 12.8g   sugar: 3g   salt: 1.1g   protein: 32.7g

beer-braised beef short ribs

prep: 20–25 mins
cook: 2 hours 35 mins–3 hours 5 mins

6 fresh thyme sprigs

6 fresh oregano sprigs

3 fresh rosemary sprigs

3 tbsp olive oil

900 g/2 lb thin ribs of beef (bone in),
   cut into 8 pieces

2 carrots, roughly chopped

1 onion, roughly chopped

2 celery sticks, roughly chopped

2 garlic cloves, crushed

350 ml/12 fl oz beer, at room
   temperature

425 g/15 oz canned tomato purée

225 ml/8 fl oz beef stock

rock salt

pepper

15 g/½ oz fresh flat-leaf parsley,
   finely chopped, to garnish

1. Preheat the oven to 140°/275°F/Gas Mark 1 and make a bouquet garni by tying the thyme, oregano and rosemary together with string.

2. Heat 2 tablespoons of the oil in a casserole over a medium–high heat. Generously season the meat all over with salt and pepper.

3. When the oil is very hot, add the ribs to the casserole, in batches to avoid overcrowding. Cook, turning occasionally, for about 8 minutes, until brown all over. Remove the ribs and pour the fat out of the casserole.

4. Add the remaining oil to the casserole and heat over a medium–high heat. Add the carrots, onion and celery and cook for about 3 minutes, until they are beginning to brown. Stir in the garlic and cook for a further minute.

5. Add the beer and bring to the boil, stirring and scraping up the sediment from the base of the casserole. Boil for 3–5 minutes, until the beer is reduced by half. Stir in the tomato purée and stock. Return the ribs to the casserole and add the bouquet garni.

6. Bring to the boil, cover and transfer to the preheated oven. Cook for 2–2½ hours until the meat is very tender.

7. Just before serving, remove and discard the bouquet garni. Serve immediately garnished with chopped parsley.

serves 4

cals: 604   fat: 33.8g   sat fat: 11.4g   fibre: 4.7g   carbs: 22.8g   sugar: 9.6g   salt: 2.6g   protein: 46.3g

texas lone star chilli

prep: 25 mins
cook: 2 hours 20 mins

2 tbsp vegetable oil

1.3 kg/3 lb stewing steak, cut into 1-cm/½-inch cubes

1 large onion, diced

3 garlic cloves, very finely chopped

2 green bird's eye chillies, deseeded and very finely chopped

2 red jalapeño peppers, deseeded and very finely chopped

2 tbsp hot chilli powder, or to taste

1 tbsp ground cumin

1 tsp dried oregano

1½ tsp salt

½ tsp pepper

¼ tsp cayenne pepper

750 ml/1¼ pints beef stock

280 g/10 oz chopped tomatoes

1 tbsp polenta

water as needed

diced white onion and freshly chopped coriander, to garnish (optional)

1. Heat the oil in a flameproof casserole or large heavy-based pan, and add the beef, in batches if necessary, over a high heat and sear until well browned. Add the onion to the pan, reduce the heat to medium and fry for 5 minutes. Add the garlic and cook for a further 1 minute.

2. Add all the remaining ingredients, except the polenta and bring to the boil. Reduce the heat to low, cover and simmer for 1 hour, stirring occasionally. Uncover and stir in the polenta. Continue cooking uncovered, stirring occasionally, for a further 1 hour or until the meat is very tender. Add some water during the cooking to adjust the thickness, if necessary, and occasionally skim off any foam that floats to the surface.

3. Taste and adjust the seasoning, if necessary. Serve the chilli immediately, garnished with white onions and coriander, if liked.

serves 4

top tip

Make this spicier by upping the
quantity of fresh chillies, jalapenos,
chilli powder and cayenne!

cals: 703   fat: 21.6g   sat fat: 5.8g   fibre: 3.7g   carbs: 17.9g   sugar: 6.3g   salt: 4.7g   protein: 108g

ham & leek risotto

prep: 20 mins
cook: 35-40 mins

380 g/13¼ oz arborio rice

1 litre/1¾ pints water

2 tbsp olive oil

350 g/12 oz cooked ham, diced

1 shallot, diced

2 leeks, white and light green parts
   only, trimmed and diced

30 g/1 oz fresh parsley, finely chopped,
   plus extra to garnish

4 tbsp dry white wine

1 litre/1¾ pints chicken stock, plus
   extra if needed

145 g/5¼ oz fresh or frozen peas

30 g/1 oz butter

60 g/2¼ oz freshly grated Parmesan
   cheese, plus extra to garnish

salt

variation

If you're not a fan of peas, use the same quantity of fresh or frozen broad beans instead.

1. Rinse the rice under cold running water. Place in a large saucepan with the water and a generous pinch of salt. Bring to the boil over a high heat, then reduce the heat to low and simmer, uncovered, for 7 minutes. Drain in a colander and set aside.

2. Heat the oil in the pan used to cook the rice. Add the ham, shallot, leeks and parsley and cook, stirring, for about 3 minutes until the vegetables begin to soften and the ham begins to brown.

3. Add the wine and cook for a further 1–2 minutes. Add the rice, stock and ¼–½ teaspoon of salt and bring to the boil. Reduce the heat to medium and simmer, stirring occasionally, for 12 minutes, or until most of the stock has evaporated.

4. Taste the risotto. If it is not yet cooked through, add a little more stock and cook for a few more minutes. Stir in the peas in the last couple of minutes of cooking. Stir in the butter and cheese, then garnish with extra cheese and parsley and serve immediately.

serves 4

cals: 737   fat: 23.6g   sat fat: 9.6g   fibre: 4.2g   carbs: 90g   sugar: 4.7g   salt: 6.6g   protein: 36.8g

chorizo with butter beans & barley

2 tbsp vegetable oil

1 onion, chopped

3 celery sticks, sliced

2 red peppers, deseeded and cut into squares

2 tbsp chopped fresh oregano

2 large garlic cloves, chopped

500 g/1 lb 2 oz chorizo sausage, thickly sliced

185 g/6½ oz pearl barley, rinsed

1 litre/1¾ pints chicken stock

400 g/14 oz canned butter beans, drained and rinsed

salt and pepper

steamed cabbage, to serve (optional)

1. Heat the oil in a flameproof casserole or heavy-based saucepan, add the onion and fry over a medium–high heat for 5 minutes.

2. Add the celery, red peppers, oregano and garlic and fry for a further 5 minutes.

3. Add the chorizo and fry for 5 minutes, turning frequently.

4. Stir in the barley and stock and season to taste with salt and pepper. Bring to the boil, then cover and simmer for about 1 hour, until the barley is tender but still slightly chewy.

5. Add the beans and simmer for 5 minutes to heat through. Serve immediately with steamed cabbage, if liked.

variation

You can replace the butter beans with chickpeas or cannellini beans, if you wish.

cals: 913   fat: 57g   sat fat: 19.5g   fibre: 13.2g   carbs: 58.6g   sugar: 5.8g   salt: 7g   protein: 40.7g

chimichurri steak

prep: 25 mins
cook: 15 mins, plus resting

675–900 g/1 lb 8 oz–2lb sirloin steak

1 shallot, finely chopped

3 garlic cloves, finely chopped

4 tbsp sherry vinegar or red
   wine vinegar

60 g/2¼ oz fresh flat-leaf parsley,
   finely chopped

1 tbsp fresh oregano leaves,
   finely chopped

½ tsp crushed red pepper flakes

125 ml/4 fl oz olive oil

juice of 1 lemon

4 fresh corn cobs,
   husks and silks removed

salt and pepper

1. Preheat the grill to medium–high. Generously season the steak with salt and pepper.

2. Place the shallot and garlic in a small bowl with the vinegar and 1 teaspoon of salt. Add the parsley and oregano along with the red pepper flakes. Whisk in the oil until well combined. Stir in the lemon juice.

3. Wrap the corn cobs individually in foil and place on the grill rack with the steak. Cook the steak, turning once, for about 4 minutes per side for medium-rare, until nicely seared on the outside. Turn the corn occasionally, cooking it for 15 minutes in total.

4. Transfer the meat to a chopping board and leave to rest for 4 minutes. Slice it against the grain into 5-mm/¼-inch thick slices. Serve the meat drizzled with the sauce and with the corn on the side.

cals: 735   fat: 51.9g   sat fat: 11.6g   fibre: 3g   carbs: 22g   sugar: 7.4g   salt: 1.8g   protein: 45.7g

get fresh or dry out?

There is a place in the kitchen for both fresh and dried ingredients — sometimes depending on time and cost, and other times depending on seasonal availability. Here we have a list of some culinary essentials of both types, that no cook should be without.

storecupboard staples

Grains

Grains such as rice, barley, oats, quinoa and bulgar wheat contain a package of concentrated nutrients. Perked up with colourful spices and herbs, they form a nutritious base to which meat, fish and vegetables can be added.

Pulses

Dried pulses are packed with nutrients, and provide a mellow background to more strongly flavoured ingredients. Canned pulses are invaluable since you can add them to the pot without soaking or precooking.

Pasta and rice

Short pasta shapes, from tiny star-shapes to coils and fat tubes, make the basis for endless one pot meals. Pasta shapes can be precooked or added to the pot with plenty of liquid. Rice is also a storecupboard must-have — use either white, brown or wild, depending on the recipe and your personal preference.

Spices and dried herbs

For the best flavour, buy spices whole (including pepper), and grind them as needed. Rosemary, thyme and oregano are the best herbs to use dried; the more delicate varieties are better when fresh. Add spices and dried herbs at the early stages of cooking to bring out the full flavour.

fresh produce

Vegetables

One of the most important source of vitamins, minerals and fibre, vegetables are packed with carotenoids (the plant form of vitamin A), vitamin C and vitamin E, which can help protect against heart disease and some cancers.

Meat and poultry

Meat and poultry provide high quality protein, important minerals such as iron and zinc, and B vitamins, needed to release energy from food. Meat tends to be high in fat, so if you're trying to cut down, trim off any excess or choose lean cuts. Try to buy meat and poultry fresh or buy frozen from a reputable butcher, where you know it has been frozen swiftly.

Fish and seafood

Dense-fleshed fish and seafood make marvellous one pot meals. They provide protein and essential minerals, while oily fish are a unique source of omega-3 fatty acids that protect against heart disease and feed the brain. Fresh is best and once purchased, should ideally be eaten on the same day. Buying fresh also means you can check for freshness and quality, such as clear, bright eyes; firm, plump flesh and the slight smell of the sea air.

Fresh herbs

A generous sprinkling of fresh herbs added at the end of cooking will provide delightful fragrance and colour to one pot meals.

large mixed grill

prep: 15 mins
cook: 27–31 mins

1 fillet steak, about 225 g/8 oz
2 small lamb chops
2 large field mushrooms
1 large beef tomato, cut in half
6 tbsp vegetable oil
2 pork sausages
1 gammon steak, about 225 g/8 oz
55 g/2 oz chorizo, sliced
2 eggs
salt and pepper
cooked chips, to serve (optional)

1. Season the fillet steak, lamb chops, mushrooms and tomato with salt and pepper to taste.

2. Heat 4 tablespoons of the oil over a high heat in a large frying pan. When the oil starts to smoke, add the lamb chops and sausages to the pan and cook the chops for 2 minutes on each side until seared and brown. Reduce the heat and continue to cook the chops until done to your liking. Remove the chops from the pan and keep warm on a large serving platter.

3. Return the heat to high and add the gammon steak and fillet steak. Cook the gammon for 3-4 minutes on each side and the fillet steak for 2 minutes on each side, or until cooked to your liking. Turn the sausages every now and then to ensure even cooking.

4. Remove just the gammon and fillet steaks from the pan and add to the platter. Add the chorizo, mushrooms and tomato and cook on each side for 4 minutes, then add to the platter, leaving the sausages in the pan.

5. Reduce the heat to medium and heat the remaining 2 tablespoons of oil in the pan. Pushing the sausages to one side, fry the eggs to your liking and add to the platter.

6. Remove the sausages from the frying pan, slicing one open to ensure that no traces of pink remain.

7. Cut the gammon and fillet steaks in half and serve the platter immediately, with freshly cooked chips, if liked.

serves 2

cals: 1310   fat: 102g   sat fat: 30.5g   fibre: 2.4g   carbs: 12.3g   sugar: 5g   salt: 7.2g   protein: 86.1g

lancashire hot pot

prep: 30–35 mins
cook: 2½ hours

900 g/2 lb best end lamb chops

3 lambs' kidneys, cored and quartered

55 g/2 oz butter

900 g/2 lb floury potatoes, such as
    King Edward or Maris Piper,
    thinly sliced

3 onions, halved and finely sliced

2 tsp fresh thyme leaves

1 tsp finely chopped fresh rosemary

600 ml/1 pint chicken stock

salt and pepper

1. Preheat the oven to 160°C/325°F/
Gas Mark 3.

2. Trim the chops of any excess fat and place
in a bowl. Add the kidneys to the bowl and
season with salt and pepper to taste.

3. Grease a large, shallow ovenproof dish or
deep roasting tin with half the butter and
arrange a layer of potatoes in the bottom.
Layer up the onions and meat, seasoning with
salt and pepper to taste and sprinkling in the
herbs between each layer. Finish with a neat
layer of overlapping potatoes.

4. Pour in most of the stock so that it covers
the meat. Melt the remaining butter and
brush the top of the potato with it. Reserve
any remaining butter. Cover with foil and cook
in the preheated oven for 2 hours. Uncover
the hot pot and brush the potatoes again with
the melted butter. Return the hot pot to the
oven and cook for a further 30 minutes, or
until the potatoes are crisp and brown.
Serve immediately.

top tip

Use a food processor with the slicing blade fitted to slice the potatoes thinly and evenly.

cals: 718   fat: 46g   sat fat: 23.3g   fibre: 5g   carbs: 31.4g   sugar: 5g   salt: 2g   protein: 46.1g

pork medallions in a creamy sauce

prep: 20 mins
cook: 15-20 mins

500 g/1 lb 2 oz pork fillet

1 tbsp olive oil

15 g/½ oz butter

1 onion, finely chopped

200 ml/7 fl oz dry cider

1 tbsp Dijon mustard

150 ml/5 fl oz crème fraîche

salt and pepper

1 tbsp chopped fresh flat-leaf parsley, to garnish

1. Trim the pork fillet of any fat, then cut into 2.5-cm/1-inch thick slices. Place between two sheets of clingfilm and beat with a meat mallet until the meat is about half its original thickness. Lightly season on both sides with salt and pepper.

2. Heat the oil and butter in a wide frying pan, add the pork slices and fry over a medium–high heat for 3–4 minutes, turning once, until golden brown. Remove from the pan, set aside and keep warm.

3. Add the onion to the pan and fry gently, stirring, for 3–4 minutes, until soft. Add the cider, stirring with a wooden spoon to scrape up any sediment from the base of the pan, then boil rapidly for about 1 minute until slightly reduced. Stir in the mustard and crème fraîche, and gently simmer, stirring, until the sauce is smooth and has thickened a little.

4. Return the pork medallions to the pan and bring the sauce back to the boil. Season to taste with salt and pepper, sprinkle with chopped parsley and serve immediately.

cals: 338   fat: 20.8g   sat fat: 11.3g   fibre: 0.9g   carbs: 6g   sugar: 2.8g   salt: 2.4g   protein: 26.9g

quick beef stew

prep: 20 mins
cook: 35 mins

900 g/2 lb sliced quick-cook
  stir-fry beef

3 tbsp plain flour

2 tbsp olive oil

1 large onion, diced

2 garlic cloves, finely chopped

225 ml/8 fl oz red wine

450 g/1 lb button
  mushrooms, quartered

450 g/1 lb new potatoes, diced

4 carrots, diced

2 celery sticks, diced

750 ml/1¼ pints beef stock

3 tbsp tomato purée

1 tbsp fresh thyme leaves,
  finely chopped

2 tbsp fresh parsley leaves,
  finely chopped

salt and pepper

toasted bread, to serve (optional)

top tip

You can use whatever vegetables are in season — or the ones you most like — in this hearty and adaptable stew.

1. Season the beef with ½ teaspoon of salt and ½ teaspoon of pepper. Toss in the flour. Heat the oil in a large, heavy-based saucepan over a medium–high heat. Add the meat and cook, stirring frequently, for about 4 minutes until brown all over.

2. Add the onion and garlic to the pan and cook for 2–3 minutes until the onion begins to soften. Add the wine and bring to the boil, scraping up any sediment from the base of the pan.

3. Add the mushrooms, potatoes, carrots and celery to the pan with 1 teaspoon of salt, ½ teaspoon of pepper, the stock, tomato purée and thyme. Bring to the boil, then reduce the heat to low, cover and simmer for about 15 minutes until the vegetables are tender.

4. Remove the lid of the pan and continue to simmer for a further 5 minutes until the sauce is slightly thickened. Stir the parsley into the pan and serve the stew hot, with toasted bread for mopping up the sauce, if liked.

cals: 719   fat: 18.2g   sat fat: 4.4g   fibre: 8.2g   carbs: 50.3g   sugar: 11.5g   salt: 3.1g   protein: 82g

pork & apple one pot

prep: 20 mins
cook: 30 mins

30 g/1 oz plain flour

675 g/1 lb 8 oz boneless pork shoulder, cut into small cubes

2 tbsp vegetable oil

1 onion, diced

4 smoked bacon rashers, diced

2 large green apples, such as Granny Smith, cored and diced

350 g/12 oz baby new potatoes, diced

225 g/8 oz green cabbage, shredded

1 tbsp fresh thyme leaves

1 tbsp white wine vinegar

475 ml/16 fl oz chicken stock

225 ml/8 fl oz apple juice

2 tbsp Dijon mustard

salt and pepper

top tip

This stew can be refrigerated or frozen. Make up a double batch and freeze half so you can have a really quick meal ready when you need it

1. Place the flour in a large polythene bag and season the pork with 1 teaspoon of salt and ½ teaspoon of pepper. Put the meat in the bag with the flour, close the top and shake to coat well.

2. Heat the oil in a large, heavy-based saucepan over a medium–high heat. Add the onion and bacon and cook, stirring, for about 3 minutes until the onion begins to soften and the bacon begins to brown.

3. Add the pork and cook, stirring occasionally, until the meat is brown all over. Transfer the mixture to a bowl.

4. Add the apple, potatoes, cabbage and thyme to the pan along with the vinegar, stock and apple juice.

5. Add the mustard, ½ teaspoon of salt and ¼ teaspoon of pepper, bring to the boil, then reduce the heat to simmering. Return the pork, onion and bacon to the pot and cook, uncovered, for about 15 minutes until the meat is cooked through. Serve immediately.

cals: 698   fat: 42g   sat fat: 13g   fibre: 6.6g   carbs: 42.5g   sugar: 14.7g   salt: 3.3g   protein: 37.8g

spring lamb stew

prep: 20 mins
cook: 1½ hours–1 hour 40 mins

40 g/1½ oz butter

2 tbsp sunflower oil, plus extra
   as needed

900 g/2 lb boned shoulder of lamb,
   trimmed and cut into large chunks,
   any bones reserved

2 shallots, finely chopped

1 tbsp sugar

1 litre/1¾ pints lamb stock

2 tbsp tomato purée

1 bouquet garni, with several parsley
   and thyme sprigs, 1 bay leaf and 1
   small rosemary sprig

8 new potatoes, such as Charlotte,
   scrubbed and halved, if large

4 young turnips, quartered

12 baby carrots, scrubbed

140 g/5 oz frozen peas

salt and pepper

chopped fresh flat-leaf parsley,
   to garnish

baguette, to serve (optional)

1. Melt 30 g/1 oz of the butter with the oil in a large frying pan over a medium heat. Add the lamb, in batches to avoid overcrowding the pan, and fry, stirring, until coloured on all sides, adding extra oil, if necessary. Transfer the meat to a large casserole as it colours.

2. Melt the remaining butter with the fat left in the pan. Add the shallots and stir for 3 minutes, or until beginning to soften. Sprinkle with the sugar, increase the heat and continue stirring until the shallots caramelize, taking care that they do not burn. Transfer to the casserole and remove any charred bits from the base of the frying pan. Add half of the stock to the pan and bring to the boil, scraping the base of the pan, then tip this mixture into the casserole.

3. Add the remaining stock, tomato purée, bouquet garni and bones, if any, to the casserole. Season to taste with salt and pepper. Cover and bring to the boil. Reduce the heat and simmer for 45 minutes.

4. Add the potatoes, turnips and carrots and continue simmering for 15 minutes. Add the peas, then uncover and simmer for a further 5–10 minutes, or until the meat and all the vegetables are tender. Remove and discard the bones, if used, and the bouquet garni. Taste and adjust the seasoning, if necessary. Garnish with parsley and serve with a baguette for soaking up the juices, if liked.

cals: 814   fat: 39.8g   sat fat: 16g   fibre: 6g   carbs: 30.4g   sugar: 11g   salt: 4.7g   protein: 82g

beef wellington

prep: 35-40 mins, plus cooling and chilling
cook: 1 hour 5 mins-1 hour 20 mins

2 tbsp olive or vegetable oil

1.5 kg/3 lb 5 oz beef fillet, cut from the middle of the fillet, trimmed of fat and sinew

55 g/2 oz butter

150 g/5½ oz mushrooms, chopped

2 garlic cloves, crushed

150 g/5½ oz smooth liver pâté

few drops of truffle oil (optional)

1 tbsp finely chopped fresh parsley

2 tsp English mustard

500 g/1 lb 2 oz puff pastry thawed, if frozen

1 egg, lightly beaten

salt and pepper

cooked vegetables, to serve (optional)

1. Place a large frying pan over a high heat and add the olive oil. Rub salt and pepper to taste into the beef and sear very quickly all over in the pan. (This method gives a rare version. If you want it less rare, roast it at 220°C/425°F/Gas Mark 7 for 20 minutes at this stage.) Remove the beef and set aside to cool.

2. Heat the butter in the frying pan over a medium heat, add the mushrooms and fry for 5 minutes. Reduce the heat, add the garlic and fry for another 5 minutes. Put the mushrooms and garlic in a bowl, add the pâté, truffle oil, if using, and parsley, and beat with a fork. Leave to cool.

3. Rub the mustard into the seared beef fillet. Roll out the pastry into a rectangle large enough to wrap the whole fillet with some to spare. Spread the mushroom paste in the middle of the pastry, leaving a 5-cm/2-inch gap between the paste and the edge of the pastry, and lay the beef on top. Brush the edges of the pastry with beaten egg and fold it over, edges overlapping, and across the meat to completely enclose it.

4. Preheat the oven to 220°C/425°F/Gas Mark 7. Place the wrapped beef in a roasting tin with the join underneath and brush with beaten egg. Leave to chill in the refrigerator for 15 minutes, then transfer to the preheated oven and bake for 50 minutes. Check after 30 minutes – if the pastry looks golden brown, cover it in foil to prevent it burning.

5. Remove the beef wellington from the oven and carve into thick slices. Serve immediately, accompanied with freshly cooked vegetables, if liked.

serves 6

cals: 1119   fat: 76.8g   sat fat: 39.3g   fibre: 2g   carbs: 31.3g   sugar: 1.9g   salt: 2.8g   protein: 74.9g

cod almighty

Make sure you buy responsibly sourced fish and seafood from trusted suppliers as many species are being depleted due to over-fishing. Check government guidelines for the latest advice.

something fishy

tuna chowder

prep: 20 mins
cook: 50 mins

2 tbsp butter

1 large garlic clove, chopped

1 large onion, sliced

1 carrot, chopped

400 g/14 oz potatoes

400 g/14 oz canned cannellini beans

600 ml/1 pint fish stock

400 g/14 oz canned chopped tomatoes

1 tbsp tomato purée

1 courgette, trimmed and chopped

225 g/8 oz canned tuna in brine,
   drained

1 tbsp chopped fresh basil

1 tbsp chopped fresh parsley

100 ml/3½ fl oz double cream

salt and pepper

fresh basil sprigs, to garnish (optional)

1. Melt the butter in a large saucepan over a low heat. Add the garlic and onion and cook, stirring, for 3 minutes, until slightly softened. Add the carrot and cook for a further 5 minutes, stirring.

2. Meanwhile, cut the potatoes into chunks and drain the beans. Pour the stock into the pan, then add the potatoes, beans, tomatoes and tomato purée.

3. Season to taste with salt and pepper. Bring to the boil, then reduce the heat, cover the pan and simmer for 20 minutes.

4. Add the courgette, tuna, chopped basil and parsley and cook for a further 15 minutes. Stir in the cream and cook very gently for a further 2 minutes.

5. Remove from the heat and ladle into warmed bowls. Garnish with sprigs of fresh basil, if liked, and serve immediately.

cals: 434   fat: 20g   sat fat: 12g   fibre: 9.2g   carbs: 39g   sugar: 10.2g   salt: 3g   protein: 24.6g

prawns in mediterranean sauce

prep: 20 mins, plus cooling and chilling
cook: 35 mins

125 ml/4 fl oz dry white wine

125 ml/4 fl oz water

6 tbsp olive oil

2 large garlic cloves, thinly sliced

1 small red onion, finely chopped

thinly pared zest of 1 large lemon

2 tbsp lemon juice

1 tbsp coriander seeds, toasted and
   lightly crushed

½ tbsp black or pink peppercorns,
   lightly crushed

pinch of dried chilli flakes, or to taste

20 raw tiger prawns, peeled and
   deveined

salt and pepper

chopped fresh flat-leaf parsley,
   dill or coriander, to garnish

sliced baguette, to serve

1. Put the wine, water, oil, garlic, onion, lemon zest and juice, coriander seeds, peppercorns and chilli flakes into a saucepan. Cover and bring to the boil over a high heat, then reduce the heat and simmer for 20 minutes.

2. Add the prawns to the liquid and simmer for 2–3 minutes, or until they turn pink. Use a slotted spoon to remove the prawns from the liquid immediately and transfer them to a deep bowl.

3. Bring the poaching liquid back to the boil, uncovered, and boil for 5 minutes, or until reduced by half. Leave to cool to lukewarm, then pour over the prawns. Season the prawns to taste with salt and pepper and leave to cool completely. Cover the bowl with clingfilm and chill for at least 4 hours.

4. When ready to serve, garnish with parsley and serve chilled, with plenty of sliced baguette for mopping up the juices.

cals: 387   fat: 27.3g   sat fat: 3.5g   fibre: 1.7g   carbs: 6.6g   sugar: 1.8g   salt: 2.1g   protein: 31.2g

prawn & chilli-lime spaghetti

prep: 15–20 mins
cook: 25–30 mins

450 g/1 lb dried spaghetti

2 tbsp olive oil

4 garlic cloves, crushed

2–4 red or green jalapeño chillies, deseeded and diced

4 small courgettes, diced

450 g/1 lb raw prawns, peeled and deveined

grated zest and juice of 1 lime

3 spring onions, thinly sliced

2 tbsp butter

salt

thyme sprigs, to garnish (optional)

1. Bring a large saucepan of lightly salted water to the boil, add the spaghetti, bring back to the boil and cook for 8–10 minutes, or until tender but still firm to the bite.

2. Drain the pasta in a colander and return the pan to the heat. Add the oil and heat over a medium–high heat. Add the garlic and cook, stirring, for 1–2 minutes until the garlic begins to soften. Add the chillies, courgettes and ½ teaspoon of salt and cook, stirring occasionally, until the courgettes are beginning to brown.

3. Add the prawns and lime zest and juice to the pan. Add the spring onions and cook, stirring occasionally, until the prawns are pink and cooked through.

4. Add the butter and the reserved spaghetti and cook, stirring, for 1–2 minutes until most of the liquid has evaporated.
Serve immediately, garnished with fresh thyme sprigs, if liked.

variation

Replace the raw prawns with cooked prawns or scallops. Add with the butter and cook until heated through.

cals: 712   fat: 18.1g   sat fat: 5.8g   fibre: 6g   carbs: 92.9g   sugar: 7.5g   salt: 2.3g   protein: 44.3g

bouillabaisse

prep: 25 mins
cook: 50-55 mins

1 kg/2 lb 4 oz selection of at least
    4 different firm white fish fillets, such
    as red mullet, snapper, sea bass, eel
    or monkfish, scaled and cleaned, but
    not skinned

100 ml/3½ fl oz olive oil

2 onions, finely chopped

1 fennel bulb, finely chopped

4 garlic cloves, crushed

1.25 kg/2 lb 12 oz canned chopped
    tomatoes

1.6 litres/2¾ pints fish stock

pinch of saffron strands

grated zest of 1 orange

bouquet garni of 2 thyme sprigs,
    2 parsley sprigs and 2 bay leaves,
    tied together with string

500 g/1 lb 2 oz live mussels, scrubbed
    and debearded

500 g/1 lb 2 oz cooked prawns, shell on

salt and pepper

baguette, to serve (optional)

1. Carefully pin-bone the fish, then cut
the fillets into bite-sized pieces. Heat the
olive oil in a very large frying pan or wide
saucepan with a lid and gently fry the onion
and fennel over a low heat for about 15
minutes, or until soft.

fact

Bouillabaisse is a famed fish stew from
Marseilles in the south of France. The classic
ingredients include fresh fish, tomatoes, olive
oil and saffron.

2. Add the garlic and fry for 2 minutes, then
add the chopped tomatoes and simmer for
2 minutes.

3. Add the stock, saffron, orange zest and
bouquet garni and bring to the boil. Simmer,
uncovered, for 15 minutes.

4. Discard any mussels with broken shells and
any that refuse to close when tapped. Add the
fish pieces, mussels and prawns and cover the
pan. Simmer for a further 5–10 minutes, or
until the mussels have opened. Discard any
that remain closed. Season to taste with
salt and pepper and remove and discard the
bouquet garni.

5. Serve immediately in warmed bowls with
some baguette, if liked.

cals: 391   fat: 20.2g   sat fat: 3.7g   fibre: 4.7g   carbs: 18.5g   sugar: 7.2g   salt: 3.5g   protein: 34.5g

tuna noodle casserole

prep: 20 mins
cook: 30 mins

1 tbsp olive oil

1 onion, diced

1 carrot, diced

140 g/5 oz button mushrooms, sliced

475 ml/16 fl oz chicken stock or
    vegetable stock

300 ml/10 fl oz canned condensed
    cream of mushroom soup

475 g/1 lb 1 oz canned tuna in brine

350 g/12 oz dried egg noodles

125 g/4½ oz panko breadcrumbs

55 g/2 oz freshly grated
    Parmesan cheese

salt and pepper

1. Preheat the oven to 200°C/400°F/Gas
Mark 6. Heat the oil in a large, ovenproof
frying pan or wide saucepan. Add the onion
and carrot and cook, stirring occasionally.

2. Add the mushrooms to the pan with
salt and pepper to taste and cook, stirring
occasionally, for 2–3 minutes until the
vegetables have begun to soften.

3. Stir in the stock and soup and bring to the
boil. Drain the tuna and add it to the pan,
breaking up any big chunks. Add the noodles
and stir to coat with the sauce. Cover the pan
and transfer to the preheated oven for about
15 minutes until the noodles are tender.

4. Preheat the grill to medium. Remove the
pan from the oven and stir the casserole well.
Sprinkle the breadcrumbs and cheese evenly
over the top and then place under the grill
for 2–3 minutes until the topping is golden
brown. Serve immediately.

top tip

For even cooking, ensure the noodles
are fully coated with sauce before
transferring the pan to the oven.

cals: 780   fat: 17.6g   sat fat: 4.9g   fibre: 6.7g   carbs: 99.3g   sugar: 6.8g   salt: 4.6g   protein: 55.7g

thai fish curry

prep: 15 mins
cook: 15-20 mins

1 tbsp oil

2 spring onions, sliced

1 tsp cumin seeds, ground

2 fresh green chillies, chopped

1 tsp coriander seeds, ground

4 tbsp chopped fresh coriander

1 tsp chopped fresh mint, plus extra to garnish

1 tbsp snipped fresh chives

150 ml/5 fl oz light coconut milk

4 white fish fillets, about 225 g/8 oz each

salt and pepper

cooked basmati rice, to serve (optional)

1. Heat the oil in a large frying pan or shallow saucepan and add the spring onions. Fry the spring onions over a medium heat until they are softened but not coloured.

2. Stir in the cumin, chillies and ground coriander seeds, and cook until fragrant. Add the fresh coriander, mint, chives and coconut milk and season to taste with salt and pepper.

3. Carefully place the fish fillets in the pan and poach for 10–15 minutes, or until the flesh flakes when tested with a fork.

4. Garnish the curry with the chopped mint and serve immediately, with cooked basmati rice on the side, if liked.

fact

Chicken is the most well-known main ingredient of this popular Thai curry. However, a firm white fish works just as well and provides a welcome and delicious change.

cals: 272   fat: 8.9g   sat fat: 4g   fibre: 1.3g   carbs: 4.8g   sugar: 1.9g   salt:1.8g   protein: 41.4g

mediterranean swordfish

prep: 15-20 mins
cook: 45 mins

2 tbsp olive oil
1 onion, finely chopped
1 celery stick, finely chopped
115 g/4 oz stoned green olives
450 g/1 lb tomatoes, chopped
3 tbsp capers
4 x 140-g/5-oz swordfish steaks
salt and pepper
fresh flat-leaf parsley sprigs, to garnish

fact

Swordfish is plentiful in the waters surrounding Sicily. This recipe comes from Palermo, Sicily's main port.

1. Heat the oil in a large, heavy-based frying pan. Add the onion and celery and cook over a low heat, stirring occasionally, for 5 minutes, or until soft.

2. Meanwhile, roughly chop half the olives. Stir the chopped and whole olives into the pan with the tomatoes and capers and season to taste with salt and pepper.

3. Bring to the boil, then reduce the heat, cover and simmer gently, stirring occasionally, for 15 minutes.

4. Add the swordfish steaks to the pan and return to the boil. Cover and simmer, turning once during cooking, for 20 minutes, until the fish is just cooked through and the flesh flakes easily.

5. Transfer the swordfish steaks to warmed serving plates and spoon the sauce over them. Garnish with the fresh parsley sprigs and serve immediately.

tilapia with chilli & tapenade

prep: 15-20 mins
cook: 15 mins

1 tbsp olive oil

4 tilapia fillets or other white
   fish fillets

4 tbsp tapenade

1 small red finger chilli, finely diced

4 tbsp freshly grated Parmesan cheese

4 tbsp dry white wine

salt and pepper

freshly cooked rice, to serve (optional)

1. Preheat the oven to 220°C/425°F/Gas Mark 7. Brush a wide, ovenproof dish with the oil.

2. Season the fish with salt and pepper to taste and place in the prepared dish in a single layer.

3. Mix together the tapenade and chilli and spread over the fish, then sprinkle with the cheese.

4. Pour the wine around the fish and bake in the preheated oven for about 15 minutes, or until the flesh flakes easily.

5. Serve the fish immediately with freshly cooked rice, if liked.

serves 4

top tip

If you're using frozen tilapia, defrost the fish in the refrigerator, not at room temperature.

cals: 306   fat: 13.8g   sat fat: 4g   fibre: 0.6g   carbs: 1.7g   sugar: 0.4g   salt: 2.6g   protein: 40.4g

calamari & prawn casserole

prep: 20 mins
cook: 16–22 mins

2 tbsp olive oil

4 spring onions, thinly sliced

2 garlic cloves, finely chopped

500 g/1 lb 2 oz cleaned squid bodies, thickly sliced

100 ml/3½ fl oz dry white wine

225 g/8 oz fresh or frozen baby broad beans

250 g/9 oz raw king prawns, peeled and deveined

4 tbsp chopped fresh flat-leaf parsley

salt and pepper

fresh crusty bread, to serve (optional)

1. Heat the oil in a large frying pan with a lid, add the spring onions and cook over a medium heat, stirring occasionally, for 4–5 minutes, until soft. Add the garlic and cook, stirring, for 30 seconds, until soft.

2. Add the squid and cook over a high heat, stirring occasionally, for 2 minutes, or until golden brown. Stir in the wine and bring to the boil. Add the beans, reduce the heat, cover and simmer for 5–8 minutes, if using fresh beans, or 4–5 minutes, if using frozen beans, until tender.

3. Add the prawns, re-cover and simmer for a further 2–3 minutes, until the prawns turn pink and start to curl. Stir in the parsley and season to taste with salt and pepper.

4. Serve the casserole immediately with fresh crusty bread, if liked.

3

fact

Combining seafood with broad beans is a classic Spanish concept.

cals: 295   fat: 9.5g   sat fat: 1.4g   fibre: 4.4g   carbs: 8.9g   sugar: 1.3g   salt: 2.5g   protein: 32.9g

pot stuff

There are many meals that, although perfectly delectable on their own can still be lifted by the addition of the perfect side or accompaniment. For the best-loved choices, look no further than the popular favourites – pasta, rice, bread and the all-time food staple winner – the humble potato.

All of these are quick and easy to prepare and cook making them ideal partners to one pot cooking when you're looking to save on time, effort – and washing up – in the kitchen. And they won't break the budget either!

But first off, let's look at a must-have for all one pot meals – a good, full of flavour home-made stock.

recipe essentials & additions

Stock – Stocks of many varieties are readily available to buy but can also be easily made at home. Vegetable stock is one of the most versatile as most dishes will always contain some sort of vegetables, so it will always go well with other ingredients. A basic recipe making 1 litre/1³⁄₄ pints can be made using 2 onions, 2 carrots, 2 leeks, 3 celery sticks, 1 bouquet garni, 1 teaspoon of black peppercorns and 1 teaspoon of salt. To make, simply peel and chop the vegetables and place in a large saucepan with the remaining ingredients. Add water to cover, bring to a simmer and cook for 1¹⁄₂ hours. Strain well before using.

Dried pasta – There's a huge amount of pastas – ranging in varying shapes, sizes and colours. Pasta is ideal for keeping in the storecupboard and makes an excellent accompaniment to many meals. It is almost foolproof to cook but to ensure perfect results firstly make sure you always bring the cooking water to a rapid boil before adding the pasta. Once in the pan, reduce the heat and cook at a steady boil. Most importantly, do not overcook the pasta, so always follow the recommended cooking time on the packet instructions.

Rice – Rice is a wonderfully useful ingredient and works perfectly as an accompaniment to a huge wealth of recipes as well as being an essential ingredient in others (such as risottos and paella). You can buy white, brown, long-grain, medium-grain, short-grain, easy-cook and wild rice. With so many varieties available, always make sure you follow the cooking instructions on the packet as different types are cooked for different lengths of time.

Bread – Bread is an absolute staple food in most parts of the world and has an almost infinite range of shapes, sizes and colours; can be cooked in varying ways using many different techniques and can include numerous delicious additions, from dried fruits to seeds and nuts. Today, shop-bought bread is exceptional but it is also surprisingly easy to make at home, either entirely by hand or with the help of a bread-making machine.

Potatoes – Potatoes are fantastically versatile and easy to work with. Whether adding the simple addition of steamed or boiled new potatoes, or much-loved buttery mashed potato, there's a guise to suit all tastes and occasions.

fish stew with cider

prep: 25-30 mins
cook: 40 mins

2 tsp butter

1 large leek, thinly sliced

2 shallots, finely chopped

125 ml/4 fl oz dry cider

300 ml/10 fl oz fish stock

250 g/9 oz potatoes, diced

1 bay leaf

4 tbsp plain flour

200 ml/7 fl oz milk

200 ml/7 fl oz double cream

55 g/2 oz fresh sorrel leaves, chopped

350 g/12 oz skinless monkfish or cod
  fillet, cut into 2.5-cm/1-inch pieces

salt and pepper

variation

You can make the same recipe using medium dry white wine instead of cider. If you can't get sorrel you can use spinach leaves, or half spinach, half basil.

1. Melt the butter in a large saucepan over a medium–low heat. Add the leek and shallots and cook for about 5 minutes, stirring frequently, until they start to soften. Add the cider and bring to the boil.

2. Stir in the stock, potatoes and bay leaf with a large pinch of salt (unless the stock is salty) and bring back to the boil. Reduce the heat, cover and cook gently for 10 minutes.

3. Put the flour in a small bowl and very slowly whisk in a few tablespoons of the milk to make a thick paste. Stir in a little more milk to make a smooth liquid.

4. Adjust the heat so the stew bubbles gently. Stir in the flour mixture and cook, stirring frequently, for 5 minutes. Add the remaining milk and half the cream. Continue cooking for about 10 minutes until the potatoes are tender. Remove and discard the bay leaf.

5. Combine the sorrel with the remaining cream. Stir the sorrel cream into the stew and add the fish. Continue cooking, stirring occasionally, for about 3 minutes, until the monkfish stiffens. Taste the stew and adjust the seasoning, if needed. Ladle into warmed serving bowls and serve immediately.

cals: 477   fat: 28.7g   sat fat: 17.7g   fibre: 2.9g   carbs: 31.1g   sugar: 5.9g   salt: 2.5g   protein: 21.7g

baked sea bass

prep: 30-35 mins
cook: 40-45 mins

500 g/1 lb 2 oz firm, waxy potatoes,
  very thinly sliced

1 large garlic clove, very finely chopped

2 onions, thinly sliced

2 tbsp olive oil, plus extra for greasing

2 whole sea bass, haddock, pollack
  or red snapper, about 400 g/14 oz
  total weight, heads removed, scaled,
  gutted and well rinsed

4 fresh thyme sprigs

½ lemon, sliced

150 g/5½ oz black olives, stoned
  and sliced

salt and pepper

lemon wedges, to serve (optional)

1. Preheat the oven to 220°C/425°F/Gas
Mark 7 and grease a roasting dish large
enough to hold the fish and potatoes.

2. Arrange the potatoes, garlic and onions
in a layer on the bottom of the dish, drizzle
over half of the oil and season with salt and
pepper. Tightly cover the dish with foil and
bake in the preheated oven for 30 minutes,
until the potatoes are almost tender.

3. Meanwhile, make three slashes on each side
of the fish and rub salt and pepper into the
slashes. Divide the thyme sprigs and lemon
slices between the fish slashes, then set aside.

4. Reduce the oven temperature to
190°C/375°F/Gas Mark 5. Uncover the dish
and stir the olives into the potatoes. Arrange
the fish on top, drizzle over the remaining oil,
return to the oven and cook for 10 minutes
per 2.5 cm/1 inch of fish thickness, or until
the fish is cooked through and the flesh
flakes easily.

5. Remove the dish from the oven. Fillet and
skin the fish and divide the fillets between
four warmed plates. Serve with the potatoes,
onions and olives, and with lemon wedges for
squeezing over, if liked.

fact

Olives offer the same health benefits as olive oil,
but with extra phytosterols, lutein and vitamins
A and E for an added anti-ageing boost.

cals: 392   fat: 14.9g   sat fat: 2.3g   fibre: 5.9g   carbs: 30.6g   sugar: 5g   salt: 3.3g   protein: 33.4g

clams in bacon, leek & cream broth

prep: 20–25 mins
cook: 20 mins

1.5 kg/3 lb 5 oz live clams, scrubbed

1 tsp butter

12 streaky bacon rashers,
  roughly chopped

200 g/7 oz leeks, sliced

1 garlic clove, finely chopped

100 ml/3½ fl oz brandy

300 ml/10 fl oz cold water

100 ml/3½ fl oz single cream

25 g/1 oz fresh flat-leaf parsley,
  finely chopped

1. Discard any clams with broken shells or any that refuse to close when tapped.

2. Melt the butter in a deep, heavy-based saucepan over a medium heat. Add the bacon and fry, stirring, for 4–5 minutes, or until crisp and golden. Using a slotted spoon, transfer to a plate lined with kitchen paper.

3. Put the leeks and garlic in the pan and cook, stirring regularly, for 5 minutes, or until softened but not browned.

4. Pour in the brandy and leave it to bubble for a minute to burn off the alcohol (brandy in a hot pan can easily flame, so take care). Add the water and stir well. Turn up the heat to medium-high and, when the water starts to boil, toss in the clams. Put on the lid and steam for 5 minutes, or until the clams have opened.

5. Take the pan off the heat. Discard any clams that remain closed. Stir in the bacon and cream. Sprinkle with the parsley and serve in warmed bowls, with a large empty bowl to collect the shells.

cals: 442   fat: 24.2g   sat fat: 10.3g   fibre: 1.1g   carbs: 8.2g   sugar: 2.5g   salt: 3.1g   protein: 32.9g

lobster, beetroot & spinach risotto

prep: 15–20 mins
cook: 30 mins

25 g/1 oz butter

2 tbsp olive oil

1 small onion, diced

280 g/10 oz risotto rice

100 ml/3½ fl oz dry white wine

5 small raw beetroots, grated

1.6 litres/2¾ pints hot vegetable
   stock or chicken stock

1 tsp grated horseradish

juice of ½ lemon

175 g/6 oz baby leaf spinach

225 g/8 oz ready-to-eat lobster meat
   or crabmeat

115 g/4 oz freshly grated
   Parmesan cheese

salt and pepper

crème fraîche, to serve (optional)

1. Heat the butter and oil in a large saucepan over a medium heat, add the onion and fry for 3 minutes. Add the rice and stir to coat with the butter and oil. Cook for a further 2 minutes. Add the wine and simmer for 2 minutes, or until absorbed.

2. Add the beetroots and stir well. Add two ladles of stock to the pan, then cover and cook for 2 minutes, or until absorbed. Stir well and add another ladle of stock. Stir constantly until the stock is absorbed, then add another ladle. Continue adding the stock, one ladle at a time, until it has all been absorbed and the rice is almost cooked.

3. Stir in the horseradish and lemon juice, then add the spinach and season to taste with salt and pepper. Divide between warmed bowls, top with the lobster meat and cheese and serve immediately, accompanied by crème fraîche, if liked.

serves 4

top tip

When grating beetroot, make sure you wear clean plastic gloves to protect your skin from staining.

cals: 611   fat: 22.3g   sat fat: 10.2g   fibre: 4.7g   carbs: 71g   sugar: 6.8g   salt: 6.2g   protein: 28.6g

paella

prep: 30-35 mins, plus soaking
cook: 45-50 mins

6 tbsp olive oil

6–8 boned chicken thighs

140 g/5 oz chorizo, diced

2 large onions, chopped

4 large garlic cloves, crushed

1 tsp mild or hot paprika

350 g/12 oz paella rice, rinsed and drained

100 g/3½ oz French beans, chopped

125 g/4½ oz frozen peas

1.3 litres/2¼ pints fish stock

½ tsp saffron threads, soaked in
  2 tbsp hot water

16 live mussels, scrubbed, debearded and
  soaked in salted water for 10 minutes

16 raw prawns, peeled and deveined

2 red peppers, halved and deseeded,
  then grilled, peeled and sliced

salt and pepper

freshly chopped parsley, to garnish

1. Heat 3 tablespoons of the oil in a 30-cm/ 12-inch paella pan or casserole. Cook the chicken over a medium–high heat, turning frequently, for 5 minutes, or until golden and crisp. Using a slotted spoon, transfer to a bowl.

2. Add the chorizo to the pan and cook, stirring, for 1 minute, or until beginning to crisp, then add to the chicken.

3. Heat the remaining oil in the pan, add the onions and cook, stirring, for 2 minutes. Add the garlic and paprika and cook for a further 3 minutes, or until the onions are soft but not brown.

4. Add the rice, beans and peas and stir until coated in oil. Return the chicken and chorizo and any accumulated juices to the pan. Stir in the stock, saffron and its soaking liquid, and salt and pepper to taste and bring to the boil, stirring. Reduce the heat to low and simmer, uncovered, for 15 minutes.

5. Discard any mussels with broken shells and any that refuse to close when tapped. Arrange the mussels, prawns and peppers on top. Cover and simmer for 5 minutes until the prawns turn pink and the mussels open. Discard any mussels that remain closed.

6. Ensure the chicken is cooked through and the juices run clear by inserting a skewer into the thickest part of the meat. Garnish with the parsley and serve immediately.

serves 6

cals: 808   fat: 42.1g   sat fat: 10.9g   fibre: 4.8g   carbs: 61.4g   sugar: 6.4g   salt: 4g   protein: 42.2g

salmon & potato casserole

prep: 25-30 mins
cook: 25-30 mins

450 g/1 lb new potatoes
2 tbsp olive oil, plus extra for oiling
1 tsp salt
350 g/12 oz Brussels sprouts
½ tsp pepper
675 g/1 lb 8 oz salmon fillet
2 tbsp unsalted butter
1 tbsp finely chopped fresh dill
juice of 1 lemon
3 spring onions, trimmed and sliced

top tip

A mandolin makes quick work of slicing the potatoes. If you don't have one, use a good, sharp knife.

1. Preheat the oven to 230°C/450°F/Gas Mark 8 and oil a large baking dish. Slice the potatoes into thin rounds and place them in the base of the dish in an even layer. Drizzle half the oil evenly over the potatoes, then sprinkle with half the salt. Place in the preheated oven.

2. Trim and thinly slice the sprouts. Put them into a medium-sized bowl and toss with the remaining oil, half the remaining salt and the pepper. Remove the dish from the oven and spread the sliced sprouts over the top of the potatoes in an even layer. Return to the oven.

3. Cut the salmon into 5-cm/2-inch chunks and season with the remaining salt. Put the butter into a small bowl and melt in the microwave. Add the dill to the butter with the lemon juice.

4. Remove the dish from the oven and place the salmon pieces on top of the vegetables. Spoon the butter mixture over the salmon pieces and drizzle any remaining mixture over the vegetables. Scatter the spring onions over the top. Return to the oven and bake for 10–12 minutes until the salmon flakes easily with a fork and the vegetables are cooked through. Serve immediately.

cals: 585   fat: 35.5g   sat fat: 9.8g   fibre: 6.4g   carbs: 27.3g   sugar: 3.8g   salt: 1.8g   protein: 40g

mussels in cider

prep: 20-25 mins
cook: 25 mins

2 kg/4 lb 8 oz live mussels, scrubbed
   and debearded
300 ml/10 fl oz dry cider
6 shallots, finely chopped
6 tbsp double cream
pepper
fresh baguettes, to serve (optional)

top tip

Straining the cooking liquid through a muslin-lined sieve is imperative as it helps remove the grit that the mussels will have naturally accumulated in the wild.

1. Discard any mussels with broken shells or any that refuse to close when tapped.

2. Pour the cider into a large casserole, add the shallots and season with pepper. Bring to the boil and cook for 2 minutes.

3. Add the mussels, cover with a tight-fitting lid and cook over a high heat, shaking the casserole dish occasionally, for about 5 minutes, or until the shells have opened. Remove the mussels with a slotted spoon, discarding any that remain closed, and keep warm.

4. Strain the cooking liquid through a muslin-lined sieve into jug, then return the strained liquid to the casserole. Bring to the boil and cook for 8–10 minutes, or until reduced by about half. Stir in the cream and add the mussels. Cook for 1 minute to reheat the shellfish, then serve immediately with fresh baguettes, if liked.

serves 4

cals: 351   fat: 16.7g   sat fat: 7.7g   fibre: 0.7g   carbs: 3.6g   sugar: 2.2g   salt: 1.8g   protein: 31g

one pot clam bake

prep: 25–30 mins
cook: 35–40 mins, plus standing

2 tbsp olive oil

25 g/1 oz butter

4 shallots, finely chopped

4 garlic cloves, chopped

4 celery sticks, finely chopped

1 tbsp smoked paprika

475 ml/16 fl oz apple cider

2 litres/3½ pints chicken stock

500 g/1 lb 2 oz new potatoes

2 corn cobs, each cut into 3

200 g/7 oz smoked sausage, sliced

1 kg/2 lb 4 oz live clams, scrubbed

1 kg/2 lb 4 oz large raw prawns, shells on

small bunch fresh parsley, chopped

salt and pepper

crusty bread, to serve (optional)

1. Add the olive oil, butter, shallots, garlic and celery to a large casserole with a tight-fitting lid. Cook uncovered over a medium-low heat for 10 minutes, or until the shallots are translucent.

2. Add the smoked paprika, cider and hot chicken stock, bring to the boil and add the new potatoes. Cover and simmer for 10 minutes, then add the corn cobs and smoked sausage. Cook for a further 10 minutes, until the potatoes are almost soft.

3. Discard any clams with broken shells and any that refuse to close when tapped. Add the clams and prawns to the casserole, and cook for a further 2 minutes, until the clams have opened and the prawns have turned pink. Discard any clams that remain closed.

4. Remove from the heat and leave for a couple of minutes, then add the chopped parsley and season with salt and pepper to taste. Transfer to a large serving dish and serve immediately with crusty bread, if liked.

cals: 701   fat: 32.3g   sat fat: 10.7g   fibre: 6.6g   carbs: 44.4g   sugar: 7.4g   salt: 10.5g   protein: 50.6g

pea brained

Don't be left in the dark about
how good vegetables are for you.
Typically, they are low in both
fat and calories and have
zero cholesterol.
They are also great sources of
vitamins A and C, plus other
important nutrients.

veg out

sweet potato & apple soup

prep: 20 mins, plus cooling
cook: 50 mins

1 tbsp butter

3 leeks, thinly sliced

1 large carrot, thinly sliced

600 g/1 lb 5 oz sweet potatoes, diced

2 large Bramley apples, peeled, cored and diced

1.2 litres/2 pints water

freshly grated nutmeg

225 ml/8 fl oz apple juice

225 ml/8 fl oz single cream

salt and pepper

snipped fresh chives or coriander, to garnish

1. Melt the butter in a large saucepan over a medium–low heat.

2. Add the leeks, cover and cook for 6–8 minutes, or until soft, stirring frequently.

3. Add the carrot, sweet potatoes, apples and water. Lightly season to taste with salt, pepper and nutmeg. Bring to the boil, reduce the heat and simmer, covered, for about 20 minutes, stirring occasionally, until the vegetables are very tender.

4. Leave the soup to cool slightly, then purée in the pan with a hand-held blender.

5. Stir in the apple juice, place over a low heat and simmer for about 10 minutes, until heated through.

6. Stir in the cream and simmer for a further 5 minutes, stirring frequently, until heated through. Taste and adjust the seasoning, if necessary.

7. Ladle the soup into warmed bowls, garnish with chives and serve.

top tip

This soup is great for using up any excess apples you may have after a good apple season.

cals: 251   fat: 9g   sat fat: 5.4g   fibre: 4.8g   carbs: 38.3g   sugar: 20.7g   salt: 1.2g   protein: 3.3g

baked pumpkin & gruyère cheese

prep: 20–25 mins
cook: 1¼ hours

1 large pumpkin
300 ml/10 fl oz double cream
3 garlic cloves, thinly sliced
1 tbsp fresh thyme leaves
125 g/4½ oz Gruyère cheese, grated
salt and pepper
crusty bread, to serve (optional)

1. Preheat the oven to 180°C/350°F/ Gas Mark 4. Cut horizontally straight through the top quarter of the pumpkin to form a lid. Scoop out the seeds. Put the pumpkin in a large, deep ovenproof dish.

2. Heat together the cream and garlic in a saucepan until just below boiling point. Remove from the heat, season to taste with salt and pepper and stir in the thyme.

3. Pour into the pumpkin and replace the lid. Bake in the preheated oven for 1 hour, or until the flesh is tender – the exact cooking time will depend on the size of the pumpkin. Take care not to overcook the pumpkin, or it may collapse.

4. Remove from the oven, lift off the lid and scatter over the Gruyère cheese. Return to the oven and bake for a further 10 minutes.

5. Serve the soft pumpkin flesh with a generous portion of the cheesy cream and crusty bread, if liked.

top tip

This dish makes a lovely starter or works beautifully as a vegetable accompaniment to roast meats.

cals: 361   fat: 30.7g   sat fat: 19g   fibre: 1.2g   carbs: 14.6g   sugar: 3.5g   salt: 1.2g   protein: 9.1g

spring vegetable frittata

prep: 20 mins
cook: 12–16 mins

15 g/½ oz pine nuts

5 eggs

55 g/2 oz fine asparagus spears

55 g/2 oz French beans

55 g/2 oz fresh shelled baby broad
  beans or peas

1 tsp olive oil

10 g/¼ oz butter

25 g/1 oz fresh Parmesan cheese
  shavings

handful of rocket leaves

salt and pepper

fresh crusty bread, to serve (optional)

top tip

You can add almost anything to the egg mixture of a frittata, making it hugely versatile. It is also equally delicious cold as it is hot and makes an ideal picnic dish.

1. Toast the pine nuts in a large, heavy-based frying pan with a heatproof handle over a medium heat, stirring until they are golden brown. Tip out onto a plate.

2. Using a fork, lightly beat the eggs in a bowl with salt and pepper to taste.

3. Preheat the grill to high. Half-fill the frying pan with water and bring to the boil. Add the asparagus, French beans and broad beans. Simmer for 2 minutes, then drain and transfer to a plate.

4. Dry the pan and return to a medium heat. Add the oil and butter and, when melted and foaming, add the vegetables and pour the beaten eggs over the top.

5. Cook the frittata for 1–2 minutes, until lightly browned underneath, then place the pan under the preheated grill and cook for 1–2 minutes, until just set in the middle.

6. Pile the Parmesan cheese shavings and rocket on top of the frittata and scatter with the pine nuts. Serve immediately with fresh crusty bread, if liked.

cals: 399   fat: 28.2g   sat fat: 9.6g   fibre: 4g   carbs: 9.7g   sugar: 3g   salt: 2.6g   protein: 26.7g

kale pesto spaghetti

prep: 20–25 mins
cook: 20 mins

225 g/8 oz kale, stems and centre
ribs removed

450 g/1 lb dried spaghetti

40 g/1½ oz toasted pine nuts

1 large garlic clove

¾ tsp salt

1 lemon

125 ml/4 fl oz olive oil

30 g/1 oz freshly grated Parmesan
cheese, plus extra to garnish

400 g/14 oz canned cannellini beans

2 tbsp chia seeds, to garnish

top tip

Freeze the pesto in small portions in an ice cube tray. Transfer the frozen cubes to a re-sealable freezer bag and use as needed.

1. Bring a large saucepan of lightly salted water to the boil and fill a medium-sized bowl with iced water. Blanch the kale leaves in the boiling water for 45 seconds. Using a slotted spoon, transfer the kale to the iced water. Bring the salted water back to the boil. Drain the kale, place it in a clean tea towel and squeeze to remove any excess water.

2. Add the pasta to the boiling water and cook for 8–10 minutes, until tender but still firm to the bite.

3. Meanwhile, combine the kale, pine nuts, garlic and ¾ teaspoon of salt in a food processor. Zest the lemon into the bowl of the processor, then halve the lemon and squeeze in the juice of one half. Pulse until smooth. With the motor running, drizzle in the oil until it is fully incorporated. Add the cheese and pulse until incorporated.

4. Drain and rinse the beans, then toss into the pasta. Immediately drain the pasta, reserving some of the cooking water. Toss the pasta and beans with the pesto. Add a little of the reserved cooking water if needed to coat the pasta nicely. Serve immediately with a generous dusting of cheese and a sprinkling of chia seeds.

cals: 930   fat: 45.9g   sat fat: 7.6g   fibre: 11.8g   carbs: 103.4g   sugar: 4.3g   salt: 1.6g   protein: 27.9g

warm vegetable medley

prep: 20 mins, plus cooling
cook: 22 mins

4 tbsp olive oil

2 celery sticks, sliced

2 red onions, sliced

450 g/1 lb aubergines, diced

1 garlic clove, finely chopped

5 plum tomatoes, chopped

3 tbsp red wine vinegar

1 tbsp sugar

3 tbsp stoned green olives

2 tbsp drained capers

salt and pepper

4 tbsp chopped fresh flat-leaf parsley,
   to garnish

fresh ciabatta bread, to serve (optional)

variation

For an indulgent cheesy-twist, gently stir 1 x 125 g/4½ oz ball of fresh mozzarella, torn into pieces, into the medley just before serving.

1. Heat half the oil in a large, heavy-based saucepan. Add the celery and onions and cook over a low heat, stirring occasionally, for 5 minutes, until soft but not coloured. Add the remaining oil and the aubergines. Cook, stirring frequently, for about 5 minutes, until the aubergines begin to colour.

2. Add the garlic, tomatoes, vinegar and sugar and mix well. Cover the mixture with a round of greaseproof paper and simmer gently for about 10 minutes.

3. Remove and discard the greaseproof paper, then stir in the olives and capers. Season to taste with salt and pepper.

4. Tip the mixture into a serving dish and leave to cool slightly. Garnish with the parsley and serve with fresh ciabatta, if liked.

serves 4

cals: 234 fat: 15g sat fat: 1.9g fibre: 7.7g carbs: 24.4g sugar: 13.3g salt: 1.7g protein: 3.5g

vegetable risotto

prep: 20 mins
cook: 35–40 mins

375 g/13 oz arborio rice

1 litre/1¾ pints water

1 fennel bulb

1 shallot

350 g/12 oz asparagus spears

2 tbsp olive oil

50 ml/2 fl oz dry white wine

1 litre/1¾ pints vegetable stock

handful of fresh parsley

2 tbsp butter

70 g/2½ oz crumbled goat's cheese

30 g/1 oz grated Parmesan cheese, plus extra to garnish

zest and juice of 1 lemon

salt

1. Thoroughly rinse the rice under cold running water. Place in a large saucepan with the water and a little salt. Bring to the boil, then reduce the heat to low and simmer, uncovered, for 7 minutes. Meanwhile, trim and core the fennel and dice the fennel and the shallot. Cut the asparagus spears into 4-cm/1½-inch pieces. Drain the rice in a colander and set it aside.

2. Heat the oil in the pan. Add the shallot and fennel and cook, stirring, for about 3 minutes until the vegetables begin to soften. Add the wine and cook for a further minute. Add the rice, stock, asparagus and a little salt and bring to the boil. Reduce the heat to medium and simmer, stirring occasionally, for about 12 minutes until most of the stock has evaporated. Meanwhile, finely chop the parsley.

3. Taste the risotto. If it is not yet cooked through, add a little more stock and cook for a further few minutes. Stir the butter, goat's cheese and Parmesan cheese into the risotto. Add the lemon zest and juice and stir to combine. Serve immediately, garnished with Parmesan cheese and parsley.

serves 4

cals: 614   fat: 23.1g   sat fat: 10.3g   fibre: 7.3g   carbs: 82.6g   sugar: 3g   salt: 4g   protein: 17.2g

cheese & tomato bake

prep: 20-25 mins, plus optional cooling
cook: 50-55 mins, plus standing

olive oil, for greasing

450 g/1 lb cherry tomatoes

85 g/3 oz goat's cheese, rind removed
if necessary, finely crumbled

2 tbsp fresh thyme leaves

55 g/2 oz plain flour

pinch of sugar

4 large eggs

300 ml/10 fl oz milk

salt

mixed salad leaves, to serve (optional)

1. Preheat the oven to 180°C/350°F/Gas Mark
4. Lightly grease a 1.5-litre/2½-pint baking
dish. Arrange the tomatoes in a single layer
in the dish, then scatter over the cheese and
thyme and set aside.

2. Sift the flour, sugar and a pinch of salt into
a large bowl and make a well in the centre.
Break the eggs into the well and use a whisk
or fork to blend them together. Add half the
milk and stir, gradually incorporating the
flour from the side of the bowl, until blended.
Whisk in the remaining milk until a smooth
batter forms.

3. Gently pour the batter over the tomatoes,
shaking the dish slightly to distribute the
cheese and thyme. Place in the preheated
oven and bake for 50–55 minutes, or until
the batter is puffed, golden and set and the
tomatoes are tender.

4. Remove the bake from the oven and
leave to stand for 5 minutes before serving.
Alternatively, leave to cool completely and
then serve with mixed salad leaves, if liked.

cals: 285   fat: 14.3g   sat fat: 6.3g   fibre: 1.9g   carbs: 19.7g   sugar: 7.5g   salt: 2g   protein: 15.7g

spicy bean chilli

prep: 20 mins
cook: 20 mins

1 large onion

1 large green pepper

2 garlic cloves

2 tbsp olive oil

2 tsp dried crushed chillies

400 g/14 oz canned chopped plum
  tomatoes

300 g/10½ oz canned red kidney
  beans, drained

300 g/10½ oz canned cannellini beans,
  drained

3 tbsp chopped fresh coriander

salt and pepper

tortilla chips, to serve (optional)

1. Chop the onion, deseed and chop the green pepper and crush the garlic. Heat the oil in a large frying pan over a medium heat. Add the onion and green pepper and stir-fry for 8 minutes until soft and light brown.

2. Stir in the garlic and chillies, then add the tomatoes and simmer for 2 minutes.

3. Add the kidney beans, cannellini beans and coriander, bring to the boil, then reduce the heat and simmer for 5 minutes. Season to taste with salt and pepper.

4. Transfer to warmed serving bowls and serve immediately with tortilla chips, if liked.

serves 4

cals: 278   fat: 8.2g   sat fat: 1g   fibre: 12.2g   carbs: 34g   sugar: 7.6g   salt: 1.5g   protein: 13g

super-green stir-fry

prep: 20 mins
cook: 10 mins

500 g/1 lb 2 oz mixed leafy greens

225 g/8 oz asparagus

5 tbsp groundnut oil

3-cm/1¼-inch piece fresh ginger, diced

½–1 fresh green or red chilli, deseeded and diced

3 large garlic cloves, thinly sliced

6 baby leeks, sliced into rounds

3–4 tbsp vegetable stock or water

2 tbsp soy sauce

½ tsp salt

small handful fresh coriander leaves

1 tsp sesame seeds

1 tbsp toasted sesame oil

pepper

boiled rice, to serve (optional)

1. Cut away the stalks and large central ribs from the greens. Slice the stalks into 1-cm/½-inch pieces. Stack the leaves and slice into ribbons.

2. Snap off the woody ends from the asparagus and discard. Chop the stems into 2-cm/¾-inch pieces. Leave the tips whole.

3. Heat a large wok over a high heat and add the groundnut oil. When almost smoking, add the ginger, chilli and garlic. Stir-fry for 30 seconds. Add the leeks, asparagus and the chopped stalks from the greens. Add stock to moisten and stir-fry for a further 2 minutes. Add the sliced leaves, soy sauce, salt and a little pepper and stir-fry for 3 minutes.

4. Stir in the coriander, sesame seeds and sesame oil and stir-fry for 30 seconds. Serve immediately with boiled rice, if liked.

serves 4

cals: 251   fat: 21.3g   sat fat: 3.5g   fibre: 5.6g   carbs: 12.4g   sugar: 2.5g   salt: 2.2g   protein: 4.9g

open season

Rediscover and work with the rhythm of the seasons in the way you shop for food and plan your meals. Get to know your local grocers and farmers' market or, if you can, indulge in the therapeutic and rewarding task of growing your own produce at home.

The fact that we have changing seasons should make us recognize the value of them more. The fact that some foodstuffs have short availability should be the very reason that makes them so special. Asparagus is a prime example; its wonderful flavour is best appreciated soon out of the ground. The home-grown season may be short, but why not eat it at its most glorious, looking to other delights when the harvest is over, while eagerly anticipating its arrival again the following year? As the spring turns into summer, we can then move on to savouring crisp green beans or sweet young carrots in their prime. Choosing what is in season and looks good on the day can make shopping much more fun and meals far more exciting.

Seasonal food is fresher and tends to be tastier and more nutritious. By relying a little less on pre-packaged foods and more on natural, home-made meals made from fresh ingredients, we are also taking steps towards a healthier lifestyle and diet. Instead of quickly consuming a takeaway meal or snacking on convenience foods in front of the television, a little exercise in the form of chopping and

stirring could make all the difference, and provide us with a more nutritious, satisfying and enjoyable eating experience too.

Changing the way we shop and eat needn't be hard work. Building a nourishing diet and making the most of fresh produce can be a lot easier than we may have allowed ourselves to believe in recent times. A good

basic storecupboard that includes spices and seasonings, olive oil, pulses, rice, pasta, flour and maybe a can or two of tomatoes will make a valuable and versatile foundation. Then simply build your menus around what fresh ingredients are best for the time of year.

Focus on the type of dish and cooking method rather than following a recipe in every detail; that way you can adapt and adjust to whatever is available. If you don't have pumpkin for your pie, for example, try sweet potato instead, or if you can't find carrots for your cake, grate in a parsnip or two. And if your basil is looking limp, replace it with some lively parsley.

Seasonal eating ensures you are consuming what is naturally good for you at the right time of year. It also benefits local producers and cuts down on the amount of food miles.

To truly experience the joys of seasonal foods and cooking, look to cultivating your own fruit and vegetables where you can. You might discover your hidden gardening talents by planting a tub or two of herbs, a small patch of potatoes, or a few rows of carrots at home.

kale, sweet potato & peanut stew

prep: 15–20 mins
cook: 35–40 mins

2 tbsp olive oil

1 large onion, sliced

1 garlic clove, crushed

2 tsp ground coriander

1 tsp ground cumin

400 g/14 oz sweet potatoes,
  cut into 2-cm/¾-inch chunks

400 g/14 oz canned chopped tomatoes

2 bay leaves

300 ml/10 fl oz vegetable stock

140 g/5 oz crunchy peanut butter

200 g/7 oz curly kale, thickly sliced

salt and pepper

55 g/2 oz salted peanuts, lightly
  toasted, to garnish

fresh crusty bread, to serve (optional)

1. Heat the oil in a large saucepan over a medium heat, add the onion and fry, stirring occasionally, for about 5 minutes, until soft but not brown. Stir in the garlic, coriander and cumin and gently fry, stirring, for about 30 seconds.

2. Stir in the sweet potatoes, tomatoes, bay leaves and stock and bring to the boil. Reduce the heat to low, cover with a lid and simmer gently for 15–20 minutes, until the potatoes are tender.

3. Stir in the peanut butter and season to taste with salt and pepper. Stir in the kale, cover and simmer for a further 5–6 minutes, stirring occasionally, until just tender.

4. Spoon into a serving dish and scatter with toasted peanuts. Serve hot, with fresh crusty bread, if liked.

cals: 510   fat: 32.7g   sat fat: 5g   fibre: 8.7g   carbs: 44.3g   sugar: 17.3g   salt: 1.9g   protein: 16.5g

parsnip layered casserole

prep: 20–25 mins
cook: 55–60 mins

3 tbsp olive oil

600 g/1 lb 5 oz parsnips, peeled
   and thinly sliced lengthways

1 tsp fresh thyme leaves

1 tsp caster sugar

300 ml/10 fl oz double cream

600 g/1 lb 5 oz tomatoes,
   thinly sliced

1 tsp dried oregano

150 g/5½ oz Cheddar cheese, grated

salt and pepper

top tip

When buying parsnips, look for firm roots with no rusty patches and no damage to the skin. Store them in a cool, well-ventilated place for up to 5 days.

1. Preheat the oven to 180°C/350°F/Gas Mark 4.

2. Heat the oil in a frying pan over a medium heat, add the parsnips, thyme, sugar and salt and pepper to taste and cook, stirring frequently, for 6–8 minutes until golden and softened.

3. Spread half the parsnips over the base of a gratin dish. Pour over half the cream, then arrange half the tomatoes in an even layer across the parsnips. Season to taste with salt and pepper and scatter over half of the dried oregano.

4. Sprinkle over half the Cheddar cheese. Top with the remaining parsnips and tomatoes. Sprinkle with the remaining oregano, season to taste with salt and pepper and pour over the remaining cream. Scatter over the remaining cheese.

5. Cover with foil and bake in the preheated oven for 40 minutes, or until the parsnips are tender. Remove the foil and return to the oven for a further 5–10 minutes until the top is golden and bubbling. Serve immediately.

cals: 715   fat: 59g   sat fat: 31.7g   fibre: 9.3g   carbs: 35.8g   sugar: 13.5g   salt: 2.1g   protein: 13.6g

vegetable stew with couscous

prep: 15 mins
cook: 15 mins, plus standing

2 tbsp olive oil
1 onion, diced
2 garlic cloves, finely chopped
225 g/8 oz French beans, cut into
   5-cm/2-inch pieces
1 orange pepper or red pepper,
   deseeded and diced
400 g/14 oz canned chickpeas,
   drained and rinsed
2 tbsp garam masala
1 tsp salt
225 ml/8 fl oz vegetable stock
400 g/14 oz canned chopped
   tomatoes with their can juices
200 g/7 oz couscous
300 g/10½ oz washed baby spinach
juice of 1 lemon
2 tbsp fresh parsley leaves

to garnish (optional)
natural yogurt
sriracha sauce
chia seeds

top tip

Buy garam masala in small quantities and keep it in a sealed jar or tin in the refrigerator. If stored correctly, it should last for up to a month or so.

1. Heat the oil in a large frying pan over a medium–high heat. Add the onion and garlic and cook, stirring occasionally, for about 5 minutes until the onion is soft.

2. Add the beans and orange pepper to the pan with the chickpeas, garam masala and salt. Add the stock and the tomatoes with their can juices and bring to the boil. Cook for about 4 minutes until the beans begin to soften.

3. Stir in the couscous and spinach, remove from the heat and cover. Leave to stand for about 5 minutes until the couscous is tender and the spinach is wilted.

4. Stir the lemon juice into the stew with the parsley. Serve hot, garnished with a dollop of yogurt, a drizzle of sriracha sauce or a sprinkling of chia seeds, if using.

serves 4

cals: 433   fat: 10.3g   sat fat: 1.4g   fibre: 10.8g   carbs: 69.1g   sugar: 9.2g   salt: 2.2g   protein: 16.2g

chilli bean stew

prep: 25 mins
cook: 36-46 mins

2 tbsp olive oil
1 onion, chopped
2–4 garlic cloves, chopped
2 fresh red chillies, deseeded and sliced
225 g/8 oz canned kidney beans
225 g/8 oz canned cannellini beans
225 g/8 oz canned chickpeas
1 tbsp tomato purée
900 ml/1½ pints vegetable stock
1 red pepper, deseeded and chopped
4 tomatoes, chopped
175 g/6 oz shelled fresh broad beans
1 tbsp chopped fresh coriander, plus
  extra to garnish
paprika, to garnish (optional)
soured cream, to serve (optional)

top tip

This dish is given a little kick from the chillies and paprika. If you're not a fan, however, it will not be a problem to omit these two elements.

1. Heat the oil in a large, heavy-based saucepan with a tight-fitting lid. Add the onion, garlic and chillies and cook, stirring frequently, for 5 minutes until soft.

2. Drain and rinse the kidney beans, cannellini beans and chickpeas and add to the pan. Blend the tomato purée with a little of the stock and pour over the bean mixture, then add the remaining stock.

3. Bring to the boil, then reduce the heat and simmer for 10–15 minutes. Add the red pepper, tomatoes and broad beans.

4. Simmer for a further 15–20 minutes or until all the vegetables are tender. Stir in most of the chopped coriander.

5. Serve the stew immediately, garnished with the remaining coriander, a pinch of paprika and a spoonful of soured cream, if using.

cals: 294   fat: 10g   sat fat: 1.9g   fibre: 11.1g   carbs: 35.1g   sugar: 7.6g   salt: 2.1g   protein: 13.1g

red kidney bean curry

2 tbsp vegetable or groundnut oil

2 tsp cumin seeds

2 onions, finely chopped

2 tsp grated fresh ginger

6 garlic cloves, crushed

2 fresh green chillies, finely chopped

2 large tomatoes, roughly chopped

2 tsp ground coriander

1 tsp ground cumin

¼ tsp ground turmeric

1 tsp garam masala

800 g/1 lb 12 oz canned red kidney beans, drained and rinsed

1 tsp palm sugar

500 ml/17 fl oz warm water

1 tsp salt

4 tbsp finely chopped fresh coriander, to garnish

natural yogurt, to serve (optional)

1. Heat the oil in a large saucepan and add the cumin seeds. When they stop crackling, add the onions and fry until they are soft.

2. Add the ginger and garlic and fry for 2 minutes. Add the green chillies, tomatoes, ground coriander, cumin, turmeric and garam masala and stir-fry for 12–15 minutes.

3. Add the red kidney beans, palm sugar, water and salt and cook for 10–12 minutes, or until the beans are soft.

4. Remove the curry from the heat and transfer to a warmed serving dish. Garnish with the chopped coriander and serve immediately with a spoonful of yogurt, if liked.

cals: 339   fat: 8.9g   sat fat: 0.7g   fibre: 15.5g   carbs: 37.3g   sugar: 8.3g   salt: 1.5g   protein: 16.3g

butternut squash & lentil stew

1 tbsp olive oil

1 onion, finely chopped

3 garlic cloves, finely chopped

2 level tbsp tomato purée

2 tsp ground cumin

1 tsp ground cinnamon

¼ tsp cayenne pepper

450 g/1 lb butternut squash flesh, cut into cubes

100 g/3½ oz brown lentils

450 ml/15 fl oz vegetable stock

juice of ¼ lemon

sea salt and pepper

to serve (optional)

finely chopped fresh coriander

flaked almonds

natural yogurt

1. Heat the oil in a large saucepan over a medium–high heat. Add the onion and garlic and cook, stirring occasionally, for 5 minutes, or until soft.

2. Add the tomato purée, cumin, cinnamon and cayenne and season well with salt and pepper, then stir. Add the squash, lentils and stock, and bring to the boil. Reduce the heat to low and simmer uncovered, stirring occasionally, for 25 minutes, or until the squash and lentils are tender.

3. Just before serving, stir in the lemon juice. Serve hot, sprinkled with the coriander and almonds, with a spoonful of yogurt on top, if using.

fact

Lentils contain high levels of soluble fibre, which studies show can help to reduce the risk of heart disease. They are also rich in protein, folate and magnesium.

cals: 206   fat: 4.7g   sat fat: 4g   fibre: 6.5g   carbs: 35.6g   sugar: 5.3g   salt: 2.6g   protein: 8.6g

vegetable cocido

prep: 20-25 mins
cook: 55 mins

2 tbsp virgin olive oil

1 onion, roughly chopped

1 aubergine, roughly chopped

½ tsp smoked hot paprika

2 garlic cloves, finely chopped

1 large red pepper, deseeded and roughly chopped

250 g/9 oz baby new potatoes, unpeeled and any larger ones halved

450 g/1 lb plum tomatoes, peeled and roughly chopped

410 g/14½ oz canned haricot beans in water, drained

150 ml/5 fl oz vegetable stock

2 sprigs of fresh rosemary

2 courgettes, roughly chopped

sea salt and pepper

top tip

If you haven't used smoked hot paprika before, check before buying as it comes in two heat strengths: hot with the strength of chilli powder or mild. Either one adds a great smoky flavour to this stew.

1. Preheat the oven to 200°C/400°F/ Gas Mark 6. Heat 1 tablespoon of oil in a saucepan over a medium heat. Add the onion and fry for 5 minutes, or until softened. Add another tablespoon of oil, then add the aubergine, and fry, stirring, for 5 minutes, or until just beginning to soften and brown.

2. Stir in the smoked paprika and garlic, then the red pepper, potatoes and tomatoes. Add the haricot beans, stock and rosemary, then season with salt and pepper. Bring to the boil, cover, turn the heat down to medium-low and simmer for 30 minutes, stirring from time to time.

3. Stir the courgettes into the stew, then cook, uncovered, for 10 minutes, or until all the vegetables are tender and the sauce has reduced slightly.

4. Remove and discard the rosemary sprig. Ladle the stew into warmed bowls and serve immediately.

serves 4

cals: 270   fat: 8.3g   sat fat: 1.1g   fibre: 14g   carbs: 40.4g   sugar: 11.8g   salt: 1.9g   protein: 9.8g

half-baked

Baking is a bit more of a 'science' than other types of cooking. To ensure a good result, make sure you follow the instructions exactly and try not to be tempted to open the oven during the baking process as this can result in a sunken end product

just desserts

Creating a dessert to enjoy doesn't have to mean spending hours mixing, baking and decorating. Here we have a veritable feast of desserts to choose from, ranging from those that need little or no cooking, to those that offer the real wow-factor.

a piece of cake

gingersnap refrigerator cakes

prep: 25 mins, plus chilling
cook: No cooking

475 ml/16 fl oz double cream

50 g/1¾ oz sugar

zest and juice of 1 lemon

36 gingersnaps, 12 broken in half

40 g/1½ oz chopped crystallized ginger, to decorate

1. Put the cream into a large bowl and whip until it holds stiff peaks. Add the sugar and the lemon zest and juice and beat until well combined.

2. Spoon 2 tablespoons of the mixture into the base of each of 6 x 225-ml/8-fl oz wide-mouthed preserving jars. Top each cream layer with 1½ biscuits arranged in a single layer.

3. Spoon another 2 tablespoons of the cream mixture on top of the biscuits, and top with another 1½ biscuits. Repeat until there are 4 layers of biscuits.

4. Finish with a layer of cream. Wipe the rims of the jars clean and seal the jars with their lids. Chill in the refrigerator for at least 4 hours.

5. Just before serving, remove the lids and sprinkle the crystallised ginger over the tops.

cals: 682   fat: 47g   sat fat: 27.7g   fibre: 1.4g   carbs: 60.4g   sugar: 35.7g   salt: 0.6g   protein: 4.2g

lemon & lime posset

prep: 15-20 mins, plus cooling and chilling
cook: 8 mins

500 ml/17 fl oz double cream

140 g/5 oz caster sugar

finely grated rind and juice of 1 large lemon

finely grated rind and juice of 1 lime, plus extra rind to serve

200 g/7 oz strawberries, hulled and halved

shortbread biscuits, to serve (optional)

1. Place the cream and sugar in a saucepan. Bring slowly to the boil and simmer for 3 minutes, stirring occasionally.

2. Remove from the heat, add the lemon and lime rind and juices and whisk well. Pour into four glasses, leave to cool then cover and place in the refrigerator for about 2–3 hours until set and well chilled.

3. Divide the strawberries and extra lime rind between the glasses and serve immediately with shortbread biscuits, if liked.

top tip

This recipe is ideal for entertaining as it can be made the day before. Add the strawberries just before serving.

pistachio & almond tuiles

prep: 25 mins, plus setting and cooling
cook: 10-15 mins

1 egg white

55 g/2 oz golden caster sugar

25 g/1 oz plain flour

25 g/1 oz pistachio nuts, finely chopped

25 g/1 oz ground almonds

½ tsp almond extract

40 g/1½ oz unsalted butter, melted and cooled

1. Preheat the oven to 160°C/325°F/ Gas Mark 3. Line two baking trays with baking paper.

2. Whisk the egg white lightly with the sugar, then stir in the flour, pistachios, ground almonds, almond extract and butter, mixing to a soft paste.

3. Place walnut-sized spoonfuls of the mixture on the prepared baking trays and use the back of the spoon to spread as thinly as possible. Bake in the preheated oven for 10–15 minutes, until pale golden.

4. Quickly lift each biscuit with a palette knife and place over the side of a rolling pin to shape into a curve. When set, transfer to a wire rack to cool.

variation

Instead of pistachio nuts, use 25 g/1 oz finely chopped and roasted hazelnuts.

popcorn marshmallow bars

prep: 15-20 mins, plus setting
cook: 5 mins

70 g/2½ oz soft light brown sugar
50 g/1¾ oz butter
25 g/1 oz golden syrup
50 g/1¾ oz sweet and salty or plain popcorn
50 g/1¾ oz dried cranberries
50 g/1¾ oz mini marshmallows

1. Line a 20-cm/8-inch square cake tin with baking paper.

2. Place the sugar, butter and golden syrup in a medium-sized saucepan and gently heat until the contents have melted. Remove from the heat.

3. Stir in the remaining ingredients and mix well. Tip into the prepared tin and firmly press down with the back of a spoon.

4. Leave to set in the refrigerator or in a cool place for about 1 hour. Cut into 10 equal-sized bars and serve.

top tip

These bars are super-easy to make and the ideal choice for a children's party.

cals: 130   fat: 5.7g   sat fat: 2.8g   fibre: 0.6g   carbs: 19.8g   sugar: 16.7g   salt: 0.1g   protein: 0.6g

compote of dried fruits

140 g/5 oz ready-to-eat dried apricots, halved

140 g/5 oz ready-to-eat prunes

140 g/5 oz ready-to-eat dried apple rings, halved

55 g/2 oz dried cranberries

500 ml/17 fl oz orange juice

2 pieces stem ginger in syrup, drained and chopped, 2 tbsp syrup reserved

whipped cream or yogurt, to serve (optional)

1. Put the apricots, prunes, apple rings and cranberries into a saucepan and pour over the orange juice.

2. Bring to the boil over a medium heat, then stir in the ginger and reserved syrup. Reduce the heat to low, cover and simmer gently for about 15 minutes until the fruit is soft.

3. Lift out the fruit with a slotted spoon and place in a serving dish. Simmer the juice, uncovered, for 3–4 minutes until reduced and slightly thickened.

4. Pour the reserved syrup over the fruit and serve warm or cold with whipped cream, if liked.

cals: 392   fat: 0.7g   sat fat: trace   fibre: 9.3g   carbs: 98g   sugar: 79g   salt: trace   protein: 3.1g

prosecco & lemon sorbet

prep: 15 mins, plus cooling and freezing
cook: 5 mins

140 g/5 oz caster sugar
100 ml/3½ fl oz water
finely grated rind and juice of 1 lemon
350 ml/12 fl oz prosecco
mint sprigs, to decorate (optional)

1. Put the sugar and water into a saucepan with the grated lemon rind and stir over a low heat until the sugar dissolves.

2. Bring to the boil, then boil for 1 minute until slightly reduced. Leave to cool, then strain through a sieve.

3. Add the lemon juice and prosecco to the lemon syrup and stir to combine, then pour into an ice cream machine and churn in the machine following the manufacturer's instructions. Alternatively, pour into a container to freeze and whisk once an hour until completely frozen.

4. Remove the sorbet from the freezer about 15 minutes before serving, then scoop into serving dishes. Decorate with mint sprigs, if using, and serve.

top tip

This ultra-refreshing and decadent dessert is also delicious topped with a few red grapes.

cals: 191   fat: trace   sat fat: trace   fibre: 0.2g   carbs: 36.8g   sugar: 36g   salt: trace   protein: 0.1g

molten chocolate cupcakes

prep: 20-25 mins, plus cooling
cook: 20 mins

175 g/6 oz soft margarine
175 g/6 oz caster sugar
3 large eggs
250 g/9 oz self-raising flour
3 tbsp cocoa powder
175 g/6 oz plain chocolate

1. Preheat the oven to 190°C/375°F/Gas Mark 5. Put 9 paper baking cases in two muffin tins.

2. Put the margarine, caster sugar, eggs, flour and cocoa powder in a large bowl and, using an electric hand-held whisk, beat together until just smooth.

3. Spoon half of the mixture into the paper cases. Using a teaspoon, make an indentation in the centre of each cake. Break the chocolate evenly into 9 squares and place a piece on top of each indentation, then spoon the remaining cake mixture on top.

4. Bake the cupcakes in the preheated oven for 20 minutes, or until well risen and springy to the touch. Leave the cupcakes to cool for 2–3 minutes before serving warm.

cals: 466   fat: 25.6g   sat fat: 7.4g   fibre: 2.9g   carbs: 52.6g   sugar: 27.6g   salt: 1.3g   protein: 7g

white chocolate rocky road

prep: 25 mins, plus setting
cook: 5-8 mins

200 g/7 oz white chocolate

70 g/2½ oz butter

100 g/3½ oz shortbread biscuits

15 g/½ oz mini pink and white marshmallows

100 g/3½ oz glacé cherries, halved

1 tbsp freeze-dried raspberries

1. Line a 20-cm/8-inch square cake tin with baking paper.

2. Break the chocolate into small pieces and cut the butter into cubes. Place both in a heatproof bowl set over a saucepan of gently simmering water and heat until melted.

3. Place the biscuits in a polythene bag, seal and gently crush with a rolling pin to make small pieces. Add to the melted chocolate mixture, then stir in the marshmallows and two thirds of the cherries.

4. Spoon the mixture into the tin, spreading evenly. Place the remaining cherries on the surface and scatter over the raspberries.

5. Leave to set in a cool place for about 1 hour. Cut into 20 squares and serve.

top tip

When melting chocolate over a pan of water, don't let the water boil or the bottom of the bowl touch the water or the chocolate will overheat and burn.

cals: 126   fat: 7.3g   sat fat: 4g   fibre: 0.4g   carbs: 14.4g   sugar: 10.4g   salt: 0.1g   protein: 1g

half time

Busy lives impact on how we eat, so taking time out to cook can often seem a chore and lead us to less healthy options in the kitchen. One pot cooking is ideal for those looking to create quick, easy and tasty meals at home and pairing these recipes with hints and tips on how to make the process even more speedy can prove invaluable.

Have a look through the list opposite for tips on how to prepare your food quickly and efficiently and introduce yourself to helpful time-saving cheats. Beginning mealtimes armed with all the cooking know-how necessary will introduce you to a happier kitchen and, ultimately, to food that you can enjoy making and then devour with pleasure.

time-saving tips

Ask for help – Don't be afraid to ask your butcher or fishmonger for help in preparing meats and fish. They can quickly remove bones, fat and skin, as well as cut and joint as you wish.

Be prepared – A sure way to cut down your cooking time is to start by reading the recipe thoroughly, gathering together all the ingredients you need and then get to work weighing, washing and chopping as the recipe requires. Then, when you come to start, you'll have everything you need at your fingertips.

Equip yourself – As well as ensuring your ingredients are prepped and ready to go, it's also essential to have all the necessary tools to hand. Before embarking upon a recipe, make sure you have the correct cooking vessel required and that other items, such as knives, are sharp and fit for purpose.

Double-up – Prepare more than you need when using frequently used ingredients such as onions and garlic. Onions can be diced, placed in a polythene bag and refrigerated for the next day. Garlic can be puréed and frozen in small teaspoon-size amounts on a tray. When frozen they can be transferred to a freezer-proof polythene bag for use whenever needed.

Chill-factor – Use frozen vegetables such as corn, peas and mixed vegetables.

Bag it – If time is really tight, opt for bagged salads, fruits and vegetables that have already been washed and prepared for you. These days you can even buy ready-to-use dairy items, such as grated cheese, if you really need it!

Can it – Use canned beans and pulses as opposed to those varieties that require soaking overnight.

Quick-cook cuts – Obviously, the smaller the item to be cooked, the quicker it will cook. Choose smaller but equally tasty cuts of meat such as cutlets, chops and fillets. Minced meats are also a time-saving winner.

chocolate marshmallow fingers

prep: 20 mins, plus cooling and chilling
cook: 6–8 mins

350 g/12 oz digestive biscuits

125 g/4½ oz plain chocolate, broken into pieces

225 g/8 oz butter

25 g/1 oz caster sugar

2 tbsp cocoa powder

2 tbsp clear honey

55 g/2 oz mini marshmallows

100 g/3½ oz white chocolate chips

variation

These fingers offer a plethora of mouth-watering ingredients but feel free to experiment by adding fruits, such as juicy raisins – or nuts, such as crunchy cashews.

1. Place the digestive biscuits in a polythene bag and, using a rolling pin, crush into small pieces. Place the chocolate, butter, sugar, cocoa and honey in a saucepan and heat gently until melted. Remove from the heat and leave to cool slightly.

2. Stir the crushed biscuits into the chocolate mixture until well mixed. Add the marshmallows and mix well, then stir in the chocolate chips. Spoon the mixture into a 20-cm/8-inch square baking tin and lightly smooth the top. Chill in the refrigerator for 2–3 hours, or until set. Cut into fingers and serve.

makes 18

cals: 276   fat: 18.8g   sat fat: 9.5g   fibre: 1.5g   carbs: 25.3g   sugar: 14.1g   salt: 0.5g   protein: 2.4g

chocolate & almond tart

prep: 25 mins, plus cooling
cook: 1–1¼ hours

125 g/4½ oz butter, diced, plus extra
  for greasing
125 g/4½ oz caster sugar
4 tsp dark cocoa powder
½ tsp baking powder
4 eggs
¼ tsp vanilla extract
2 tbsp Strega, Marsala or orange juice
125 g/4½ oz plain chocolate, very
  finely chopped
200 g/7 oz ground almonds
icing sugar, for dusting

fact

Almonds are higher in calcium than almost any other plant food, making them an excellent addition to vegan diets and those that don't eat dairy products.

1. Preheat the oven to 180°C/350°F/Gas Mark 4. Grease a 20-cm/8-inch loose-based round cake tin and line with baking paper.

2. Put the butter and sugar into a large bowl and beat with an electric hand-held mixer until smooth and creamy. Sift in the cocoa powder and baking powder and beat them in, then add the eggs, one at a time, beating until each is incorporated before adding the next. Beat in the vanilla extract and Strega.

3. Add the chocolate and ground almonds and stir. Pour the mixture into the prepared tin and level the surface.

4. Bake in the preheated oven for 1–1¼ hours, or until firm to the touch and a skewer inserted into the centre comes out clean.

5. Leave to cool for 5 minutes in the tin, then remove from the tin and transfer to a wire rack to cool completely.

6. Just before serving, generously dust the top with icing sugar.

cals: 461   fat: 34.5g   sat fat: 13.4g   fibre: 4g   carbs: 30.4g   sugar: 23.9g   salt: 0.5g   protein: 10.1g

lavender shortbread

prep: 25 mins, plus chilling and cooling
cook: 30-35 mins

115 g/4 oz butter, softened, plus extra
  for greasing
55 g/2 oz lavender caster sugar, plus
  extra for sprinkling (see top tip)
140 g/5 oz plain flour
25 g/1 oz cornflour

top tip

To make lavender sugar, mix 900 g/2 lb caster sugar with 4 teaspoons of clean and dry lavender flowers. Store in an airtight jar for up to 6 months.

1. Lightly grease a baking sheet. Place the butter in a bowl. Sift over the caster sugar (reserving the lavender flowers left in the sieve) and beat together with a wooden spoon until light and fluffy.

2. Sift over the flour and cornflour and add the reserved lavender. Gradually work the flours into the creamed mixture to form a crumbly dough. Gather the dough together with your hands and knead lightly until smooth. Wrap the dough in clingfilm and chill in the refrigerator for 20 minutes.

3. Place the dough on the baking sheet and, using clean hands, press it out to an 18-cm/7-inch circle. Smooth the top by gently rolling a rolling pin over the mixture a couple of times. Crimp around the edge and mark into eight triangles with a sharp knife.

4. Preheat the oven to 160°C/325°F/Gas Mark 3. Sprinkle the dough with a little more lavender sugar. Chill in the refrigerator for at least 30 minutes until firm. Bake in the preheated oven for 30–35 minutes until just pale golden.

5. Leave the shortbread on the sheet for 10 minutes, then transfer to a wire rack to cool completely before serving.

cals: 205   fat: 12g   sat fat: 7.4g   fibre: 0.7g   carbs: 22.6g   sugar: 7g   salt: 0.2g   protein: 2.2g

mexican wedding cookies

prep: 30 mins, plus cooling
cook: 20–25 mins

225 g/8 oz butter, softened

1 tsp vanilla extract

50 g/1¾ oz icing sugar, sifted, plus extra for dusting

280 g/10 oz plain flour, sifted

100 g/3½ oz pecan nuts or walnuts, finely chopped

1. Preheat the oven to 190°C/375°F/Gas Mark 5. Line two baking trays with baking paper.

2. Place the butter and vanilla extract in a mixing bowl and beat until pale and creamy. Beat in the icing sugar until fully combined.

3. Gradually beat in the flour and the chopped nuts until just combined, taking care not to overwork the dough.

4. Use a teaspoon to remove 35 x 10-g/¼-oz pieces of dough, then roll each piece into a small sausage shape, tapering the ends slightly. Shape each one into a crescent and place on the prepared trays, flattening gently with the palm of your hand. Bake in the preheated oven for 20–25 minutes, until just starting to turn golden and crisp at the edges. Watch them carefully to ensure they don't burn.

5. Remove from the oven and leave to cool on the trays for 1–2 minutes, then transfer to a wire rack to cool completely. Generously dust with icing sugar and serve.

top tip

These cookies can also be shaped into little balls and flattened slightly before cooking. They'll keep for several days stored in an airtight tin in a cool place.

cals: 102   fat: 7.3g   sat fat: 3g   fibre: 0.5g   carbs: 8.4g   sugar: 2g   salt: 0.1g   protein: 1.1g

rice pudding

prep: 15 mins, plus optional cooling
cook: 35 mins

1 large orange
1 lemon
1 litre/1¾ pints milk
250 g/9 oz short-grain rice
100 g/3½ oz caster sugar
1 vanilla pod, split
pinch of salt
125 ml/4 fl oz double cream
brown sugar, to serve (optional)

top tip

Rather than using brown sugar, you can also try a spoonful of your favourite jam or a spoonful of honey to top your pudding.

1. Finely grate the rinds from the orange and lemon and set aside. Rinse a heavy-based saucepan with cold water and do not dry it.

2. Put the milk and rice in the pan and bring to the boil over a medium heat. Reduce the heat to low and stir in the caster sugar, vanilla pod, orange and lemon rinds and salt, and simmer, stirring frequently, until the pudding is thick and creamy and the rice grains are tender: this can take up to 30 minutes, depending on how wide the pan is.

3. Remove and discard the vanilla pod and stir in the cream. Serve at once, sprinkled with brown sugar, if using, or cool completely. The pudding will thicken as it cools, so stir in a little extra milk, if desired, before serving.

cals: 612   fat: 23.3g   sat fat: 14g   fibre: 2g   carbs: 87.5g   sugar: 38.4g   salt: 1g   protein: 12.4g

fruit & sunflower seed cookies

prep: 20-25 mins, plus cooling
cook: 12-15 mins

85 g/3 oz unsalted butter, softened, plus extra for greasing

85 g/3 oz light muscovado sugar

1 egg, beaten

225 g/8 oz plain flour

½ tsp freshly grated nutmeg

55 g/2 oz sultanas

30 g/1 oz sunflower seeds

demerara sugar, for sprinkling

1. Preheat the oven to 200°C/400°F/Gas Mark 6. Lightly grease a large baking sheet.

2. Put the butter and muscovado sugar into a mixing bowl or food processor and beat together until soft and fluffy. Add the egg and beat thoroughly, then stir in the flour, nutmeg, sultanas and sunflower seeds, mixing evenly to a fairly soft dough.

3. Break off small pieces of the dough and use your hands to roll them into walnut-sized balls. Arrange the balls on the prepared baking sheet and press to flatten slightly.

4. Sprinkle the cookies with a little demerara sugar and bake in the preheated oven for 12–15 minutes, or until golden brown. Transfer to a wire rack to cool.

cals: 128   fat: 5.6g   sat fat: 2.9g   fibre: 0.6g   carbs: 17.9g   sugar: 7.4g   salt: trace   protein: 2.2g

sicilian ice cream cake

prep: 25 mins, plus freezing and standing
cook: no cooking

400 g/14 oz ricotta cheese
175 g/6 oz icing sugar
1 tsp orange flower water
200 ml/7 fl oz double cream
100 g/3½ oz mixed peel, chopped
55 g/2 oz candied angelica, chopped
55 g/2 oz glacé cherries, chopped
40 g/1½ oz plain chocolate, chopped
40 g/1½ oz pistachio nuts, chopped
glacé fruits, to serve (optional)

variation

This delightful cake is a feast to both the eyes and the senses. You can serve with a mixture of fresh fruits if you prefer, such as cherries, grapes, blueberries and strawberries.

1. Press the ricotta through a sieve into a bowl using a wooden spoon.

2. Stir in the icing sugar and orange flower water, beating until smooth.

3. Whip the cream until thick enough to hold its shape, then fold into the ricotta mixture.

4. Churn the mixture in an ice-cream maker following the manufacturers' instructions. Alternatively, pour into a freezerproof container and freeze, uncovered, until slushy.

5. Fold in the mixed peel, candied angelica, glacé cherries, chocolate and pistachio nuts.

6. Tip the mixture into a 1.2-litre/2-pint bombe mould or pudding basin and freeze until firm. Leave at room temperature for 10–15 minutes before turning out.

7. Cut the ice cream cake into wedges and serve immediately with glacé fruits, if liked.

cals: 420   fat: 22.6g   sat fat: 13g   fibre: 1.5g   carbs: 47g   sugar: 39g   salt: 0.1g   protein: 7.4g

blueberry clafoutis

prep: 20 mins
cook: 30 mins

25 g/1 oz butter, softened, plus extra for greasing

125 g/4½ oz caster sugar

3 eggs

60 g/2¼ oz plain flour

250 ml/9 fl oz single cream

½ tsp ground cinnamon

450 g/1 lb blueberries

icing sugar, for dusting

single cream, to serve (optional)

variation

Replace the blueberries with 450 g/1 lb stoned sweet cherries, lightly poached in a little water with 1 tablespoon of sugar added.

1. Preheat the oven to 180°C/350°F/Gas Mark 4. Grease a 1-litre/1¾-pint baking dish.

2. Put the butter in a bowl with the caster sugar and beat together until pale and creamy. Add the eggs and beat together well. Sift in the flour, then gradually stir in the cream followed by the cinnamon. Continue to stir until smooth.

3. Arrange the blueberries in the base of the prepared baking dish, then pour over the batter. Transfer to the preheated oven and bake for about 30 minutes, or until puffed and golden.

4. Remove from the oven, dust lightly with icing sugar and serve immediately with cream, if using.

cals: 486   fat: 22.9g   sat fat: 12.8g   fibre: 3.1g   carbs: 63.1g   sugar: 46.5g   salt: 0.3g   protein: 9.8g

baked ring doughnuts

prep: 30 mins, plus cooling
cook: 32–47 mins

225 g/8 oz self-raising flour

1½ tsp baking powder

175 g/6 oz caster sugar

½ tsp salt

150 ml/5 fl oz milk

2 eggs, beaten

½ tsp vanilla extract

40 g/1½ oz butter, melted, plus extra
   for greasing

sugar coating
4 tbsp caster sugar
2–3 tsp ground cinnamon

1. Preheat the oven to 190°C/375°F/Gas Mark 5. Grease a six-hole doughnut tin.

2. Sift together the flour and baking powder into a bowl and stir in the sugar and salt. Make a well in the centre. Mix together the milk, eggs, vanilla extract and butter and pour into the well. Mix until smooth.

3. Spoon the mixture into a large piping bag fitted with a plain nozzle. Pipe some of the mixture into the prepared tin, filling each hole about two-thirds full. Bake in the preheated oven for 10–15 minutes, or until risen, golden and just firm to the touch. Leave to cool in the tin for 5 minutes, then turn out onto a wire rack. Bake the remaining mixture in the same way, rinsing and greasing the pan each time, to make 16 doughnuts in total.

4. To make the sugar coating, mix together the sugar and cinnamon on a plate. Gently toss each warm doughnut in the cinnamon sugar to coat completely. Serve warm or cold.

cals: 147   fat: 3.6g   sat fat: 2g   fibre: 0.6g   carbs: 26g   sugar: 15.2g   salt: 0.8g   protein: 2.6g

index